TRANSLATING CHAN

Translating Change explores and analyses the impact of changes in society, culture and language on the translation and interpreting process and product. It looks at how social attitudes, behaviours and values change over time, how languages respond to these changes, how these changes are reflected in the processing and production of translations and how technological change and economic uncertainty in the wake of events such as the COVID-19 pandemic and Brexit affect the translation market.

The authors examine trends in language change in English, French, German, Italian and Spanish. The highly topical approach to social, cultural and language change is predominantly synchronic and pragmatic, based on tracking and analysing language changes and trends as they have developed and continue to do so. This is combined with an innovative section on developing transferable translation-related skills, including writing and rewriting, editing, abstracting, transcreation and summary writing in view of a perceived need to expand the skills portfolio of translators in a changing market and at the same time to maximise translation quality. Each chapter features Pause for Thought/activity boxes to encourage active reader participation or reflection.

With exercises, discussion questions, guided further reading, a glossary of key terms and substantial support material, including tasks and career-orientated activities available at www.routledge.com/9780367683252, this innovative textbook is key reading for both students and translators or interpreters, in training and in practice.

Ann Pattison FITI is an ISO 17100:215 qualified translator, who first learned her skills as an in-house translator–abstractor with Fisons Ltd. She has taught at the University of Surrey, London Metropolitan University and Imperial College London, and is a former Senior Lecturer in Translation at the University of Westminster. Ann is now a freelance translator/author and a tutor with Translator Training. She is co-author of *Thinking English Translation* (2017) and of *Translation: A Guide to the Practice of Crafting Target Texts* (2019).

Stella Cragie is a Qualified Member of the Institute of Translation and Interpreting (MITI) and an ISO 17100:215 qualified translator. For many years she was a Principal Lecturer in Translation at the University of Westminster, where she remains a Visiting Lecturer. She is also a freelance translator and co-author of, among other texts, *Thinking English Translation* (2017) and *Translation: A Guide to the Practice of Crafting Target Texts* (2019).

TRANSLATING CHANGE

Enhanced Practical Skills for Translators

Ann Pattison and Stella Cragie

Routledge
Taylor & Francis Group

LONDON AND NEW YORK

Cover image: © Getty Images

First published 2022
by Routledge
4 Park Square, Milton Park, Abingdon, Oxon OX14 4RN

and by Routledge
605 Third Avenue, New York, NY 10158

Routledge is an imprint of the Taylor & Francis Group, an informa business

© 2022 Ann Pattison and Stella Cragie

British Library Cataloguing-in-Publication Data
A catalogue record for this book is available from the British Library

Library of Congress Cataloging-in-Publication Data
Names: Pattison, Ann, author. | Cragie, Stella, author.
Title: Translating change : enhanced practical skills for translators / Ann Pattison, Stella Cragie.
Description: London ; New York : Routledge, 2022. | Includes bibliographical references and index.
Identifiers: LCCN 2021048157 | ISBN 9780367683245 (hardback) | ISBN 9780367683252 (paperback) | ISBN 9781003136903 (ebook)
Subjects: LCSH: Translating and interpreting--Social aspects. | Language and culture. | Linguistic change. | Translating and interpreting--Study and teaching. | Translating and interpreting--Problems, exercises, etc. | LCGFT: Textbooks.
Classification: LCC P306 .P378 2022 | DDC 418/.02--dc23/eng/20211221
LC record available at https://lccn.loc.gov/2021048157

ISBN: 978-0-367-68324-5 (hbk)
ISBN: 978-0-367-68325-2 (pbk)
ISBN: 978-1-003-13690-3 (ebk)

DOI: 10.4324/9781003136903

Typeset in Bembo
by Taylor & Francis Books

Access the Support Material: https://www.routledge.com/9780367683252

CONTENTS

ACKNOWLEDGEMENTS

The authors and publisher would like to thank the following translators, interpreters and institutions for giving up their time to answer our queries and/or interview questions: Zoe Adams Green (MIL), Paul Boothroyd (MITI), Zoé Brill Diderich (BA, DPSI, MIL), (Lecturer in Interpreting, University of Westminster), Dr Lindsay Bywood (Senior Lecturer in Translation, University of Westminster), Claudia Forero (MA), Philippe Galinier (MA, MCIL, MITI), Emma Gladwell (MA, FITI), Sarah Gudgeon (BA Hons., CertTEFL), Dr Hayley Harris, Susanne James (MA, MCIL, FHEA), Steph Kantorski (MA), Kari Koonin (BA, FITI), Tim Morgan (MA, ACA), Kirsty Heimerl-Moggan (MA, FHEA, FITI), (Senior Lecturer in Conference Interpreting, University of Central Lancashire), Susan M. Neve (BA, CIOL, Dip. Trans), Mike Orlov, Executive Director of the National Register of Public Service Interpreters, Amelia Naranjo-Romero (MA, DPSI, RPSI, MCIL, MAPCI, MAIT), Frances Parkes (Max Your Voice), Nick Rosenthal (FITI), Dr Akiko Sakamoto (Senior Lecturer in Japanese Language and Translation, University of Portsmouth), Dr Brigitte Scott, Claudia Strachan (MA), Lucy Teasdale (BA) and others who preferred to remain anonymous. All their contributions were invaluable and provided us with remarkable insights into the professional languages sector, past and present.

INTRODUCTION

Writers, translators and interpreters encounter new words and changing patterns of discourse on a regular basis as part of their work, whether the words relate to informal speech, such as buzz phrases, conversations or speeches, or to specialist terminology, concepts and **texts**. Words hold a great fascination for people who make their living from written and spoken language, which adapts chameleon-like to positive and negative events, innovations, discoveries, attitudes and behaviours. The rich seam of sociocultural variation and change at any point in time is ideal material for exploration and analysis, particularly at the present time due to events of global and regional significance relating to health, the environment, politics, society, culture, geographical and historical factors. The resulting lexical melting pot, which never ceases to simmer and threatens to boil over at times, is emblematic of the way we live our lives, of the internal and external factors that affect society and of the way we communicate in speech and writing, which may be through increasingly sophisticated technologies or well-established ones, such as the print media.

In this book, we broadly respond to **four lines of enquiry**:

1. How social attitudes, behaviours and values change over time.
2. How language in general and individual languages respond to these changes.
3. How these changes are reflected in the processing and production of translations.
4. How technological change and economic uncertainty in the wake of events such as the COVID-19 pandemic and Brexit might affect the translation and interpreting market. As language professionals, we increasingly need to be experts in analytical thinking and develop enhanced transferable skills that will both maximise our professional status and potentially provide additional or even alternative career pathways.

DOI: 10.4324/9781003136903-1

Our focus combines elements from various subject areas, with the objective of:

- identifying factors that influence the development of society and culture;
- noticing how changes in society influence writing and speech (content, discourse and style);
- looking at how translators and interpreters absorb, process and respond to the challenges created by new concepts, experiences, situations and language;
- understanding how translators and interpreters can benefit from a wider range of transferable skills.

Investigation of these factors reveals a wide range of formal, specialist and informal language emerging from across the spectrum of written and oral discourse, highlighting the changes and developments in concepts and language that translators and interpreters deal with every day.

We examine trends in language change, mainly in English, with reference to French, German, Italian and Spanish. The basic principles we outline are relevant to a far wider audience. We have therefore tailored our approach and our analytical model to identifying and evaluating new, altered or repurposed lexical forms, providing a useful tool for linguists working with any language combination.

It is important to consider not only emerging lexis but also existing lexical and grammatical forms indicative of a writer's idiolect, which may reflect both new lexical trends and a certain predilection for words that are currently less popular, noting that while certain words may decline and eventually disappear from common use altogether, others may come back into fashion and be 'resurrected' or repurposed with an altered or expanded meaning and **context.** We also look at the impact of lexical decline and 'dated' language on translation and re-translation.

We combine the theme of sociocultural and language change with two innovative final chapters, which aim to develop transferable translation-related skills, including writing and rewriting, editing, abstracting, transcreation and summary writing in view of a perceived need to expand the skills portfolio of language professionals in a changing market and at the same time maximise output quality. The focus is on enhancing skills and market preparedness and on the need for analytical thinking that can help readers to offer a wider range of services to clients.

The book is structured as follows:

Chapter 1 (*Drivers of change*) introduces and discusses social and cultural change and provides an overview of transformations in values and attitudes while outlining aspects of language variation and change.

Chapter 2 (*Exploring language change and the implications for translation*) examines a range of texts from areas that exhibit particular and/or specific sociocultural changes, such as the working environment, science and technology, politics, culture and the environment. We also look at how different types of discourse adapt to sociocultural changes and explore the implications for translation and introduce our Quick Identification Guide and Guidance Table, based on the analytical model we developed for *Thinking English Translation*.

Chapter 3 (*Translating and commentary writing*) has a pragmatic focus, with opportunities to assess how new and emerging lexis is treated by translators, both in terms of research and in the translation process and product, using our specially designed analytical model to chart these changes. We provide translations of texts drawn from various types, with the common factor of new lexis and/or references to evolving social and cultural factors (or previous changes and lexical life cycles).

The comments and annotations produced by our team of translators in connection with the texts they translate in this chapter show how to develop a coherent and focused approach to translation tasks. You will also be able to get to grips with translating texts featuring challenges that reflect emerging concepts and lexis in English and in the languages we cover.

In **Chapter 4** (*Transferable skills*) we give an overview of other skills that translators and interpreters can offer to clients or potential employers, together with tips and insights from colleagues on how to approach these activities. From in-depth conversations with experienced practitioners and from publications such as the *ITI Bulletin*, we have perceived a need to expand the skills portfolio of language professionals in a changing market and at the same time explore how they can maximise the quality of their work. Our focus in this chapter is therefore on the development of transferable translation-related skills, which can have the added advantage of enhancing the standard of work that readers produce. By acquiring the ability to identify the linguistic features of a source text and take into account changes in usage, a theme which runs throughout the book, readers will have already begun to enhance their aptitude for analytical thinking. They can then apply this skill to tasks such as editing, linguistic **revision** or review, or to scanning, abstracting and summary writing, activities which can be either monolingual or bilingual.

In **Chapter 5** (*Secrets of professional success: riding the wave of changing times*) we explore new ways of working. Transferable skills certainly encompass advanced IT skills, such as familiarity with CAT tools and machine translation systems, and with remote interpreting, but these areas are evolving so fast that it would not be possible to go into detail due to their complexity. Our overall approach is based on an analytical methodology and the enhancement of practical translation skills, rather than exploring technical skills. So, in order to provide our readers with a comprehensive hands-on view of technological and commercial developments in the industry, we decided to talk to some professional translators and interpreters, and to a translation agency. These practitioners described the linguistic and social changes they have seen over their careers, shared their views of current trends and outlined their experiences with CAT tools and machine translation (MT). We also wanted to know how they saw the future of translation and the role of human translators. With their help, we have also recommended publications and sources that can provide ongoing up-to-date information on developments in the field of online databases, translation memory and computer translation systems. Furthermore, one of the activities for Chapter 5 includes a very simple post-editing task that most readers should be able to try out with their language pair. Our colleagues recommended some of the main resources they found helpful for research and stressed the importance of a translator's ability to rationalise. Between them, they provided some valuable practical tips and shared their secrets of success. Their comments provide valuable food for thought for both new and established translators and interpreters.

Each chapter contains waypoints, called **Pause for Thought**, which encourage you as language professionals to engage with analysis and discussion in an open and practical forum. We also include structured tasks, such as discussion and evaluation (open-ended or as part of group work), translation and re-translation, commenting, editing and post-editing, writing and rewriting, summarising, abstracting and transcreation. These tasks feature, for example, glossary-building exercises (in Chapter 3) that encourage you to track and identify instances of evolving terminology in texts from different decades and in various languages, and to compile your own corpus of key terms in your source and target languages. Some of the tasks set out in the 'Pause for Thought' boxes are designed to make you aware of the need to check the reliability of online information sources and of the inherent dangers of fake news or false facts.

The **expected learning outcomes** are as follows:

1. Developing an awareness of changes in attitudes, behaviour, ethics, culture and society through discussion of language change trends and analysis of texts written for general and specialist, adult and younger audiences.
2. Gaining an understanding of how such changes affect translation strategies, through analysing and exploring evolving trends in culture and society, literature, translated literature, and in language, both in source and target texts.
3. Acquiring the ability to use analytical models to investigate how language reacts to changes in culture and society, to gain a greater understanding of source texts in different genres, and to develop and implement appropriate and creative strategies for tackling translation challenges.
4. Acquiring linguistic research and glossary-building skills by gaining experience of advanced internet searching techniques, learning how to locate relevant background information and model texts in a specific academic, literary or scientific field and then identifying and extracting key new or 'repurposed' terms for use in a bilingual or multilingual glossary and checking how reliable the data source is.
5. Understanding that transferable skills are key to future-proofing your career prospects and reflecting on how to enhance the portfolio of professional services you can provide.
6. Becoming aware of evolving working practices in the various branches of the translation and interpreting sector and understanding how language professionals can adapt to change and adopt a proactive approach to their career progression.

An eResources facility is provided at www.routledge.com/9780367683252 to stimulate further discussion of the practical material featured in this book. On the site you will find activities designed for both group and independent work. They include glossary-building tasks relating to language change, gender-inclusive language, COVID-19 terminology and neologisms. Links are given to articles relevant to the inclusive language debate in Germany, which readers can use to look for similar resources in other languages. Links to additional texts illustrating social and linguistic change in Spanish and other languages are provided for readers to analyse and use to create term banks.

For career development, we provide a skills checklist that readers can use to audit their skills and plan their CPD and professional portfolios over the next five years. For the benefit of both language professionals already working in the sector and new entrants to the profession, we have included the two questionnaires sent to translators and interpreters prior to the interviews. The questions we asked and additional comments from the interview respondents should stimulate reflection and/or discussion of the optimum career pathway for each individual.

To give readers the opportunity to add to their transferable skills, we also include further editing and summary-writing tasks.

1

DRIVERS OF CHANGE

1 What factors drive change?

Changes occur continually in every aspect of our lives: some we believe to be necessary; some we consider to be beneficial; others we view with suspicion and anxiety. If we are the drivers of change, we may be optimistic and enthusiastic about the outcome; if we are urged to make changes by others or are subjected to changes we often find them unwelcome and may resist them. When we are not affected by major events in our private space or working environment we are less conscious of change, but when disruptions occur with wide-ranging effects we cannot help but take note, as we inevitably become involved in the consequences. The pace of change may be swift, lengthy or gentle; the reasons for change and the outcomes it triggers are sometimes predictable but also unexpected. In this chapter we consider some of the factors that trigger change and how language and languages react to it.

There are numerous theories about social and cultural change, some of which date back to antiquity, others to more recent times. The *Encyclopaedia Britannica* defines social change in the field of sociology as: "The alteration of mechanisms within the social structure, characterized by changes in cultural symbols, rules of behaviour, social organizations, or value systems" (www.britannica.com/topic/social-change).

As David Newman and Jodi O'Brien (2013: 442) comment in *Exploring the Architecture of Everyday Life*:

> The difficulty of pinning down any aspect of society when change is so rapid has led sociologists to study change itself. Following in the footsteps of (Émile) Durkheim, they ask: What causes all these technological, cultural, and institutional changes? On occasion, massive social change—from the private lives of individuals to entire social institutions—can result from a single dramatic

DOI: 10.4324/9781003136903-2

historical event, such as the attacks of September 11, 2001 or Hurricane Katrina. We can be thankful that such colossal events are relatively rare.

They add: "Sociologists who focus on change, however, tell us that change is more likely to be caused over time by a variety of social forces, including environmental and population pressures, cultural innovation, and technological and cultural diffusion". (https://uk.sagepub.com/sites/default/files/upm-binaries/23953_Page_442.pdf).

Émile Durkheim developed the concept of sociology (with Karl Marx and Max Weber) which eventually led to the discipline of modern social science based on "the beliefs and models of behaviour instituted by the collectivity" (cited in the Project Gutenberg eBook *The Elementary Forms of the Religious Life* by Durkheim: eBook 41360). Durkheim considered institutions as the basis of society and identified **social factors** as well as the crucial role that culture plays in society.

More specifically, seven factors can be identified that cause sociocultural change. These are: physical factors (e.g. disasters, wars) that affect the location and size of populations; economics (means of production); ideas and ideologies; cultural diffusion (where cultures are affected by others, notably in the way they dress, speak, behave, affecting industry, politics, religion, education, transport and communications); science and technology; politics (the state and government impose rules and social patterns); and education (considered the most powerful means of influencing society; www.yourarticlelibrary.com/philosophy/7-major-factors-that-influences-socio-cultural-changes/84824).

While society at large is always changing, you are probably aware of some specific or cultural changes that stand out and have triggered words or phrases in your source and target languages in the last few decades that have 'stood the test of time' and become well established. Recent events have made us all much more aware of the external and internal pressures that lead to change in society, culture and on language as a consequence.

PAUSE FOR THOUGHT 1

As an ice breaker, can you think of some changes that have influenced your attitudes and behaviour and the effects of these changes on your mother tongue?

A good example of the way change can trigger a language response can be seen in the plethora of neologisms and mixed compounds that emerged in response to the Brexit phenomenon, following the UK's vote to leave the European Union in 2016. We learn from the BBC that a video installation by artist Simon Roberts contained two parts of

> an 80-minute video of a newsreader reciting an alphabetised list of words and phrases related to Brexit; and a projection of the teleprompter he's reading.

The effect is overwhelming … For two years Roberts scoured social media and news media to make note of nearly 5,000 new expressions describing some aspect of Brexit. Early on he noticed an infusion of technical terms, and then a flowering of political soundbites. There was also a clustering of expressions around specific events, such as the July 2018 Brexit plan agreed at the Chequers country house [the summer residence of the Prime Minister]. This gave rise to, among many other phrases, "Chequers Blueprint", "Chequers Checkmated", "Chequers Euro-fudge" and "Chuck Chequers".

(www.bbc.com/culture/article/20190314-how-brexit-changed-the-english-language)

There is, apparently, no end to the British love of transforming and adapting language, whether for journalistic, humorous or political reasons. The British press produced some amusing Brexit cartoons at the time: one showed a baby being christened "Remoana" (a *Remoaner* was the Brexiteers' derogatory pun on *Remainer*, namely someone opposed to leaving the EU who did not accept the result of the Brexit referendum in 2016, combined with *moan*). Another cartoon depicted a man and woman at odds over Brexit, with the man saying "It's Bregret" and the woman "It's Regrexit". The caption below reads "A nation divided" (featured in *The Penguin Book of Brexit Cartoons* 2018: pp. 59 and 101).

Given that the 'Chequers compounds' relate to a very specific moment and event, it is unlikely that they will persist, but the future of the word Brexit will depend on how important this decision turns out to be in future. In 20 years' time it may just be another 'historical reference'!

1.1 Examples of sociocultural change

Language changes caused by sociocultural phenomena are very diverse. One of the factors involved is contact with other communities, which occurs as the influence of a culture or civilisation spreads. Latin, for instance, had an impact on English and other languages and is still used internationally in anatomy and in binomials – the system of biological nomenclature introduced by Carl Linnaeus, a Swede, in the 1750s to ensure that names assigned to newly discovered species remained consistent. The first word, which is capitalised, denotes the genus and the second, which is lower case, refers to the species (www.britannica.com/science/binomial-nomenclature). This system has proved useful not only to international scientists but also to translators. When working on texts in fields such as botany or horticulture, it enables you to double-check that you have rendered a plant name accurately.

To quote a different example, some words from Arabic date back hundreds of years and became established in many languages, such as English (*algebra, alcohol, admiral,* etc). Words and phrases are 'borrowed' (or adapted morphologically and semantically) from other cultures and language communities when there is inadequate lexis and expression in the host language to describe a new trend, concept or phenomenon (for example, a scientific or technical innovation or discovery) or where the lexis relates to domains where one language is perceived by another to be culturally desirable or superior (for example, French for gastronomy, diplomacy and fashion). This phenomenon is termed **cultural diffusion**. Some earlier historical loan-words from Italian are less than complimentary (*imbroglio, Mafia/ mafioso, Camorra*) but more recent ones show the positive cultural influence of coffee-shop culture in *barista* and *latte* (the English **reduction** of the compound *caffelatte*) and *panini* (a plural form used mainly to indicate a single sandwich in English). Such is the 'contagion' of *barista* that the ending *-ista* has spread to other words, like *fashionista*. There is possibly a clue here that Milan has for some time supplanted Paris as the capital of fashion. German, too, has made its mark in areas such as the humanities. English, along with some other languages, has absorbed German compound nouns, such as *Schadenfreude* (taking pleasure in someone else's misfortune) and *Weltanschauung* (view of the world), which encompass complex ideas that do not have straightforward one-word equivalents in many other languages. Other commonly used borrowings from German include *Angst* (fear), *Blitzkrieg* (lightning war), *Doppelgänger* (double), *Gestalt* (form or shape), *Leitmotiv* (recurrent theme) and *Realpolitik* (a politics of pragmatism). More examples can be found at: https://resources.german.lsa.umich.edu/vokabeln/deutschhilftenglisch and there is a very extensive list, at https://en.wikipedia.org/wiki/List_of_Germa n_expressions_in_English, which is arranged into categories according to subject areas or fields of discourse.

Another important driver of sociocultural change is the economy. For example, the occupation by the French of Algeria and migration to the French mainland in the 1960s was in part due to a labour shortage in France. The collapse of French colonial power led to a flow of workers from the Maghreb (north Africa) and an influx of Arabic words entered the French language as a result. Many of these words derive from Maghrebi Arabic or adapted forms, such as *bled* (from the Arabic *bilad* meaning country, which is also used to refer to a place of origin); *kif-kif* (meaning 'the same'), *clebs* (from *kelb*/dog), *chouia* (from *chouya*/a little), *toubib* or *tabeeb* (doctor) (source: www.connexionfrance.com/Mag/Language/12-Arabic-words-used-in-French). An absorbing account of this process appears in *Le Gone du Chaâba* (Shanty-Town Kid), a childhood memoir by Azouz Begag, who grew up in a shack with no electricity or plumbing yet later became France's first government minister of North African origin. The introduction by Alec G. Hargreaves, one of the translators, explains how France's post-war economic boom led to more North Africans settling in France on a long-term basis. As the economy began to suffer under the oil crisis in the 1970s, it was too late to send these workers home as they had already put down roots in France.

Physical factors can also cause sudden changes to the way we live and the language we use to describe emerging and ongoing phenomena. Take the recent coronavirus pandemic, which catapulted societies and cultures worldwide into abrupt and substantial changes of direction, adjustments and adaptations in a bid to tackle the threat of the virus – the impact of which has been social, economic, scientific, technological and cultural, in addition to the obvious serious consequences for public health. The emergence of a new strain of coronavirus (labelled

COVID-19) followed by a series of new variants of the virus has forced many businesses to reconsider and 're-engineer' their practices, adapting their working practices (such as *WFH – working from home, social distancing* and relying to a much greater extent on interactive platforms such as Zoom and Microsoft Teams for virtual meetings). In the UK, it was reported in late August 2020 that only 34% of British white-collar workers had returned to the office, compared with 83% in France and an average of 68% among their major European counterparts, so this could mark a long-term change in working practices, with knock-on effects on commuter numbers and the café culture (*The Guardian Weekly*, 25 September 2020, p. 36).

Society needs to react fast when emergencies arise. However, the speed of response to events also depends on the political and economic climate in any given time and place. Catastrophic events with a widespread reach may cause, at least temporarily, a certain levelling of society where populations are affected by new rules, novel concerns and unforeseen dangers; some try to help those most in need and to protect the vulnerable, prioritising others rather than themselves, while other people react against measures they consider to be repressive.

Emerging events affect codes of behaviour within a culture and a new phenomenon tends to trigger a response: the need for social distancing led to the avoidance of physical contact when greeting one another, replaced by the touching (or bumping) of elbows. These behaviours reflect Marshall McLuhan's famous phrase "The medium is the message", of which the colourful rainbow is also emblematic: this image, created by children and displayed in windows at the height of the pandemic, showed support for the National Health Service (NHS) in Britain during the first lockdown and expressed the public's gratitude for the dedication of healthcare and frontline workers. Similar demonstrations of support and gratitude took place worldwide.

Once 'new' behaviours become standardised, a state of **new normal** exists, taking over from the *status quo ante* (note the grammatical change of *normal* where *new* remains an adjective while *normal* functions as a noun). Yet *new normal* is quickly 'turned on its head' in the title of an article in the *Antiques Trade Gazette* – "The normal new" where *normal* has reverted to an adjective and *new* is nouned (Antiques Trade Gazette 2020: 26). Romance languages often calque new 'buzz phrases' in English where feasible (French: *nouvelle normalité*; Italian: *nuova normalità*; Spanish: *nueva normalidad*) sometimes with the addition of speech marks to signal a new form. German, on the other hand, fluctuates between the nominal form *die neue Normalität* and the loan phrase *das new normal*. In an article published online on 7 October 2020 about the introduction of a 10 p.m. *Sperrstunde* or curfew in pubs and restaurants, the *Frankfurter Allgemeine Zeitung* uses the former, with inverted commas to indicate that it is a neologism (www.faz.net/aktuell/rhein-main/frankfurt/sperrstunde-in-frankfurt-ein-weiter-weg-zur-neuen-norma litaet-16989279.html, accessed on 22.10.20). Not content with *new normal*, this phrase has already morphed and reduced into *new norm*, particularly in informal discourse, driven by the tendency in English to shorten and abbreviate words to speed up communication.

Grammatical change is a technique that English uses with ease due to the simplicity of its grammar and **syntax**. The technique is often used in advertising, where innovative use of language, both lexical and grammatical, aims to capture the attention of readers or viewers. Examples of this strategy include: "Your search for a place beyond *ordinary* is over" (advert for a cruise line from www.macmillandictionaryblog.com); "Give the gift of *happy* this Xmas" or "*Quick, safe and reliable* is right at your fingertips" (taxi company) (source: www.stackexchange.com/questions/305305/is-there-a-term-for-the-use-of-adjectives-as-nouns). The last example is of particular interest, as no less than three adjectives are 'nouned'. To start with, the reader assumes that these words are adjectives and therefore a noun will follow, rather than a verb. The unusual sequence attracts attention and forces the reader to engage with a string of words in order to make sense of the message. The process of **nouning** (or **nominalisation**) is defined quite simply as: "the use of another part of speech as a noun" by the Oxford English Lexico site (www.lexico.com/definition/nouning). What is more, according to Lexico, the term appears to date back to the mid-18th century (the earliest use is found in work by Elizabeth Griffith, 1727–1793, playwright and writer).

A well-known example of deliberately 'corrupt' language is the comment by Alice "Curiouser and curiouser" (in Lewis Carroll's children's classic *Alice's Adventures in Wonderland*). The unusual use of the *-er* comparative with a three-syllable adjective imitates the kind of mistake a child might make as they struggle to understand the use of the English comparative forms. An early Italian translation of this phrase attempts to convey the singularity of the language by creating a nonsensical superlative/comparative/superlative form: "'Curiosissimo e sempre più curiosissimo!' gridò Alice", (translated by Teodorico Pietrocola-Rossetti in the 1872 Italian edition) (https://it.wikisource.org/wiki/Le_avventure_d%27Alice_nel_paese_delle_meraviglie/II).

But how low can modern-day copywriters stoop to stand out from the crowd? What are we to make of a recently seen advert at a railway station, depicting a large bottle of sauce with the wording KETCHUP – BUT GOODER. Is it really necessary to distort what little remains of English grammar to attract the public's attention? Is it comical and trendy, or just blatant attention-grabbing? Worse still, might this mutilated form catch on? Online research identifies this ketchup as one of a series of condiments produced by a company called Rubies in the Rubble, whose ethical credentials (fighting food waste by using discarded fruit and vegetables) are no doubt noble, but the language 'hook' used to draw in the public is less than noble....

Sometimes genuine **hypercorrections** occur with comparatives of monosyllabic adjectives, such as more + -er (e.g. more faster). Puns are also popular in advertising, such as *Souper* for Baxters soups. It is little wonder that **transcreation** (transposing the message to adapt it to the **target culture/s** rather than 'translating it') is such a difficult task.

PAUSE FOR THOUGHT 2

If you translate from English, how would you deal with the nouned forms in italics in the examples above and the incorrect comparative of 'good'? Is it possible in your target language to replicate these forms?

Group work: How effective, in advertising terms, do you think these adapted forms are in English?

---

2 Changing values, attitudes and behaviour

2.1 Cultural issues

A localised event that turned into an outpouring of public anger across the world in 2020 was the killing of George Floyd in Portland, Oregon. The question of racial origins and perceived inequality has long been a subject of passionate debate and Floyd's demise at the hands of a white American police officer was the spark that lit the fire of revolt, initially in the United States, then in many other countries in solidarity with the Black community. Black Lives Matter (BLM) is now a movement with global resonance that has caused many individuals and institutions to reconsider their approach to, and understanding of, race and history. For example, cultural institutions in the UK and elsewhere found it necessary to re-examine their mission statements. The National Trust states, "We have a duty to play our part in creating a fairer, more equitable society" and "Though we recognise a need to improve experiences for a broader ethno-cultural audience and the people of colour who work or volunteer with us, we know that we must also look at other areas of our provision". One focus is interpretation, which is the way a public or private cultural institution narrates its history, its collections, and the lives of the people who lived or worked in a particular context.

Increased sensitivity to adjusting cultural orientation has raised some awkward questions. The National Trust considers whether the change in attitude is "just a knee-jerk reaction to Black Lives Matter" but concludes, "We have been doing this work for a number of years because legacies of colonialism and slavery are a real part of the historic fabric in our hands" (de Souza 2020). Wellcome Collection goes even further, as Melissa Gronlund (2020) writes in *The i Newspaper*:

> Under its new director, Melanie Keen, it has committed to addressing its "foundation of white supremacy", as it explained in a statement responding to the Black Lives Matter protests. Already in 2018 Wellcome Collection allocated £1m to address implicit racial, class and gender biases in the workplace, putting training in place to help staff of colour navigate micro-aggressions and instances of racism. Support is also going to the visitor experience team who

work in the library and exhibition spaces. The museum is also being reposi-
tioned to give voice to the communities from whom the artefacts were taken.

(Gronlund 2020)

A change in attitude to the way we refer to the Black Community is evident in the
decision taken by the Associated Press (the parent company of *The Guardian* newspaper)
to always use a capital letter B when using the word Black. The change conveys "an
essential and shared sense of history, identity and community among people who
identify as Black, including those in the African diaspora and within Africa", comments
John Daniszewski, AP's vice-president of standards. "The lowercase black is a color, not
a person" (www.theguardian.com/media/2020/jun/20/associated-press-style-guide-
capitalize-black). Interestingly, some sources have also called for 'white' to have an initial
capital letter. While these physical changes may be small in themselves, they reflect an
increasing momentum for greater respect towards non-white ethnic groups in general
and greater sensitivity to issues of race and diversity. An article in *le Monde* on 19 June
2020 also adopts the convention of capitalisation in French in the headline to a news
item on the European Parliament's resolution that the slave trade was a crime against
humanity (*La vie des Noirs compte*: www.lemonde.fr/international/article/2020/06/19/
la-vie-des-noirs-compte-proclame-le-parlement-europeen-dans-une-resolution_60435
20_3210.html, accessed on 18.09.20).

Changing attitudes in cultural institutions generate new, revisited or repurposed
lexis in terms of approach, interpretation, research and staff training, such as some
phrases in the Wellcome change text above and others, for example: *decolonising
collections, the idea of anti-blackness* and *colonialist legacies*. Recent events, including the
COVID-19 epidemic, have opened a Pandora's box of challenges in the way that
institutions such as museums and galleries manage their collections, raising
uncomfortable questions about how objects might have entered a public collection,
how they are narrated, examined and interpreted, and on the restitution of cultural
objects, all of which requires directors and curators to "rigorously trace acquisitions
back to their origins and investigate the dark side of how museums come to own
certain objects", as Melissa Baksh (2020) comments in a book review on exploring
and explaining "how to actively question the colonial histories of the objects and
works of art in our collections".

PAUSE FOR THOUGHT 3

The following text describes an exhibition at a modern art gallery featuring
Grace Jones (actress, pop star, model, artists' muse).

Nottingham Contemporary's upcoming exhibition – a cross between fan-fic-
tion, study and biography – seeks to question Black image-making, and our
reading of the iconic star, while reflecting the multiplicity of her persona. In
1979, her collaborator and then-partner Jean-Paul Goude made mouldings of
her face, producing a so-called "armada of Grace". An interesting departure

point, it is also a way to think of Jones in artistic terms, as a "multiple" of her own design. The exhibition will present a fractured picture of a figure who has spent a career exploring and exploding binary and facial stereotypes – and one who, at 72, continues to demand our attention.

Which words or phrases in the text do you think indicate new language and cultural trends in presenting exhibitions? If you translate from English, are translations of these words (and concepts) readily accessible in your target language? If you translate into English, write a brief summary of the exhibition text in your source language.

Sensitivity to matters of race and history has been on the increase for many years, albeit gradually to start with. About 15 years ago, one of the authors was asked to translate an exhibition catalogue for a Swiss museum displaying a series of items from a private collection of African art (figural wood carvings). Before the translation was commissioned, the author of the text wanted to see whether the translator was able to use appropriate vocabulary and language for this specialist area. The word 'appropriate' meant not only specialist terms for the subject (such as *coiffure* for the way a sculpture's hair is styled or *scarification* for skin decorations made using sharp tools), but also concepts that needed to be handled sensitively – for example, an ethnic community was to be rendered as a *people* or *group* not as a *tribe*, which has colonialist overtones. The author also made a distinction between *art* (ritual items of recognised quality) and *craftwork* (items made for commercial reasons, especially for tourists), reflecting a move away from considering all artefacts made in developing countries as 'folk art'. However, in the art and antiques business some auction houses continue to refer to sales of African or Oceanic artefacts as *Tribal Art*, while a more culturally appropriate title preferred by other players in the market is *Ethnographica*. Some earlier ethnographic cultural labels are now undesirable as they smack of colonialism, such as *Eskimo* (now Inuit) and *Ashanti* (referring to the language or people of Ghana), now referred to as Assante.

If you translate texts from the very wide fields of the arts and social sciences, you should note that the social and cultural 'labels' currently preferred may have changed and you should always check for the most appropriate vocabulary in your target language for culturally-sensitive references.

Incidentally, the word *tribe* is also used more generally, and increasingly to indicate a social group: as Nigel Morris (2020) writes, "Historic political divisions between left and right are breaking down as class barriers erode, with Britons falling into one of seven 'tribes'" (i.e. progressive activists, civic pragmatists, disengaged battlers, established liberals, loyal nationals, disengaged traditionalists, Backbone Conservatives).

Nadeau and Barlow examine the effects of French colonisation of the Caribbean and of settlement in North America on the French language (2008: 94–95). It not only led to new words being assimilated into French but also, due to the development of French Creoles, separate languages created during the slave trade period.

Social change for its part appears to occur at different rates in different cultures and there are many ways language can be manipulated to perpetuate an illiberal or post-liberal status quo. Many translators are not aware of the politics of language although this area was explored in depth by Clark and Ivanič in *The Politics of Writing* (1997). In an interview in the May–June 2020 issue of the *ITI Bulletin*, Radhika Menon explained that translations into Indian languages can sound literal rather than natural because "in India language reflects hierarchical issues like gender, caste and class biases" and "names of professions are also caste-related".

PAUSE FOR THOUGHT 4

Can you imagine what categories the *seven tribes* above refer to in Nigel Morris's article quoted above, without the help of the definitions produced by the think-tank that coined them? While the words themselves are unexceptional, the novel compounds create translation challenges. Can you define these challenges? If you translate from English, how would you approach the conceptual and lexical challenges? (See Bibliography p. 149 for the weblink.)

The language and depictions of colonialism in earlier fiction and comic-strip books for children and young adults (such as Tintin and Corto Maltese) have been criticised in recent years due to what some quarters consider to be offensive content. Hergé's second book – *Tintin au Congo* (Tintin in the Congo, published in 1930) – was the subject of an appeal in a Belgian court which upheld a ruling in 2011 against the plaintiffs – a Congolese immigrant and the Belgian Council of Black Immigrants – who had wanted the book banned. The Belgian court ruled that the comic strip was not racist, according to France 24 (www.france24.com/en/20121206-tintin-congo-not-racist-belgian-court-rules), despite the fact that Hergé himself had recognised that *Tintin in the Congo* was "a 'youthful sin' that reflected the prejudices of the time". Hergé also edited some of the text in 1946, to mitigate potentially offensive content. Attempts to ban the book in France were also unsuccessful. The translators of the English version (published in 2005 by Egmont UK Ltd and currently available online and in bookshops in the UK) prefaced their translation with the foreword:

> In his portrayal of the Belgian Congo, the young Hergé reflects the colonial attitudes of the time. He himself admitted that he depicted the African people according to the bourgeois, paternalistic stereotypes of the period – an interpretation that some of today's readers may find offensive. The same could be said of big-game hunting.
>
> (Tintin in the Congo, *2016*)

The Italian comic strips written and illustrated by the cosmopolitan author Hugo Pratt (born Ugo Eugenio Prat of Venetian descent) portrayed the dashing and fiercely independent adventurer Corto Maltese. Pratt's *Ballata del Mare Salato* (Ballad of the Salty Sea, published in 1967) was the first of 12 comic strips that he would write and illustrate. The story is set in Oceania and depicts ethnic groups ranging from westerners (British, Dutch, German, Italian) to Japanese and Maori. Set at the outbreak of WWI, the story also focuses on the aspirations of Melanesian peoples to be independent. Corto Maltese is the classic libertarian, and as Riccardo Capoferro points out in the article "Individual Soldier: Corto Maltese e l'immaginario coloniale". (www.academia.edu/22879147/Individual_Soldier_Corto_Maltese_e_limmaginario_coloniale), Corto is anti-imperialist and encourages the aspirations to independence of the Oceanic ethnic groups portrayed in the story. Notwithstanding this stance, the illustrations depict what we would consider today to be caricatures of certain ethnic groups, which some readers would no doubt find offensive and at odds with Maltese's principles.

One of the authors of our book was recently commissioned to translate two of Pratt's Corto Maltese books – the Ballad of the Salty Sea being one of them. While the illustrations were helpful as visual clues to the logistics, action and progression of the storyline, the physical features of the indigenous peoples referred to above were unambiguously exaggerated, causing the translator to send her own disclaimer to the client, which also covered some of the 'demeaning' language used in the comic. Translators are often unaware what use translated material will be put to, thus creating a further level of uncertainty about how to deal with potentially sensitive source text material.

A typical ethical issue that may arise can be seen in the 2020 edition of *The Ballad of the Salty Sea* by EuroComics.US, which has published several Corto Maltese titles (translated for the 2020 edition by Dean Mullaney and Simone Castaldi). Overall, the translation is well done, with the translators producing an accurate and amusing English version. In terms of 'political correctness' the translation usually strikes an appropriate balance. However, comic strips use some extreme language as standard, given that storylines are 'thrilling adventures' in exotic locations with 'baddies' and bold, brave heroes indulging in fighting and derring-do. Therefore, offensive language (such as insults) is common fodder in this genre. A particular challenge for translators, though, is how to deal with source text references to indigenous characters that today might easily be construed as racist or demeaning. Tension arises between conveying the tone of the source text and striking a balance of present-day correctness as the attitudes of yesteryear – both in the setting of the story (1914) and the date of writing (1967) – are very different from present-day attitudes. Ways of referring to individuals or groups that were once acceptable are now often considered to be offensive.

Some examples from the translation show how tough decision-making can prove to be. The utterance "There's a white officer with some colored sailors" stands out (*The Ballad of the Salty Sea*, 2020:14). Wikipedia, in its discussion of the term *colored*, points out that the word is considered offensive in British English; but in the USA, where the term originated in the mid-19th century, the situation appears rather different with some circles seeing it as outdated but not offensive (https://en.wikipedia.org/wiki/Colored). If so, audience response to use of the word in the UK and the USA may well differ. Another example from the translation occurs where Corto Maltese himself addresses a native directly as *macchia di catrame* (literally – and unpleasantly – transposed as *tar spot* in the US translation; *ibid:* 20). Confusingly, Corto comes over in the story as sympathetic to the native populations of Oceania, thus one can only assume that Pratt considered this epithet as 'jocular' in the context! Pity the poor translators – but the rendering probably makes some readers squirm with embarrassment....

Comic books are currently enjoying a resurgence. On 7 January 2021, Jim Milliot reported in *Publisher's Weekly* that sales of graphic novels had gone up by 29% during 2020. They first achieved popularity in the US through the work of the underground movement artist Kim Deitch and in the UK, Posy Simmonds recreated Flaubert's classic French novel in cartoon format as Gemma Bovary in 2000. Her work even made it to the big screen. As screens jostle for position with books, the written word now finds itself competing with images, as is demonstrated by the growing popularity on social media of emojis, which represent an example of semiotics (or communication through signs and symbols) in everyday use. The graphic novel format is also used by American cartoonist Art Spiegelman in a true and painful story that relates conversations with Art's father, Wladek Spiegelman, a Polish Jew who survived the Holocaust. The book, which presented considerable challenges to its translators, is famous for its depiction of the different races and nationalities as animals and its original title is actually the German word Maus instead of the English Mouse. In 2008, two Italian researchers, Raffaella Baccolini and Federico Zanettin, explored various translations of this work in *The Language of Trauma: Art Spiegelmann's Maus and its Translations* and in 2020, a chapter entitled "The Challenges of Translating Art Spiegelmann's Maus" by Martin Urdiales-Shaw appeared in *The Palgrave Handbook of Holocaust Literature and Culture* (pp. 511–528).

Using *politically correct* language (defined as "displaying progressive attitudes, especially in using vocabulary which is intended to avoid any implied prejudice": *Collins English Dictionary – Essential Edition*, 2nd ed., 2019) while no doubt desirable in some contemporary circles, may well be difficult to implement in translation as we have seen, due to the context, cultures and periods of the storyline, where tensions emerge between faithfully conveying authorial content and current perceptions of what is morally acceptable and suitable for present-day audiences. In fact, changes in attitudes, behaviour and perceptions towards content and language that may cause offence are very real challenges for translators, who need to consider the social and ethical issues relating to translation commissions of texts from earlier times depicting different attitudes, in addition to all the usual challenges. Sometimes a disclaimer may not be enough to assuage the concerns of a translator....

In addition to a plethora of new words and forms emerging in the wake of recent social changes, there is a move in journalism to replace words likely to offend with others that are more neutral. For example, the *Daily Mail* reports that in the wake of the Black Lives Matter movement, the BBC held a training session using an 'avoiding racial bias webinar' with their sports commentators to update them on words and phrases "which they must avoid during the new season" (Wilkes 2020). The reason given is that the following words and phrases (with suggested alternatives in brackets) are linked to slavery: *cakewalk* (a walk in the park), *nitty gritty* (the basic facts), *uppity* (agitated). Other 'banned' words are *blackballed*, *blacklisted* and *black mark*.

PAUSE FOR THOUGHT 5

Group work: If you were approached with a request to translate a literary text in which some representations of the characters are rather 'insensitive', would you accept the job? If you were prepared to accept it, what discussions would you have with the client (or intermediary) about the cultural and ethical implications of the translation, if no specific **translation brief** had been provided?

In the Corto Maltese translation examples cited, if you had to edit the comic strip for publication, would you leave the translators' versions as they are or delete any offensive renderings? Or would you take a different approach? If so, what?

2.2 Politics, ideology and gender awareness

Political events, such as the French Revolution, the Russian Revolution, the introduction of Prohibition in the United States in 1920, the rise of fascism, the end of the Cold War, the fall of the Berlin Wall, German union/reunification, 9/11 (the September 11, 2001 attacks) or Brexit also drive changes and affect the lexicon we use to describe them and the consequences of these movements. In *The Translator's Handbook* (2006: 54) Morry Sofer outlines some of the difficulties encountered by Russian translators that resulted from the end of the Cold War – they had to find Russian equivalents for unfamiliar capitalist concepts such as finance, insurance and legal issues due to the "transformation of the Russian language from a tool of Communist propaganda to a free-market economy language".

Although the above event acted as a driver of language change, there are sometimes factions within specific language areas that try to rein in language change. Academies such as the *Académie Française* (created in 1635) and champions of linguistic purism, such as the 17th-century lawyer and poet François Malherbe and his contemporary Cardinal Richelieu, played an active role in resisting language change, according to Nadeau and Barlow in *The Story of French* (2008: 64). The French academy has also been fighting against terms such as *Madame la ministre,* which entered the French language through the efforts of some high-profile female politicians after the Socialists won the 1997 Legislative elections (*ibid:* 367). The academy still insists on using *Madame le ministre*, the masculine article being considered to convey neutrality. Traditionally, *Madame la ministre* referred to the minister's wife rather than to a woman occupying the position.

A similar battle has raged over *Madame la juge* but according to https://business. toutcomment.com/article/on-dit-madame-le-juge-ou-madame-la-juge-13369.htm l (accessed on 17.09.20), it is preferable to address a female judge as *Madame le juge*. This site recommends *Madame le préfet, Madame le sous-préfet* and *Madame le maire* but also *Madame l'ambassadrice*. Similar anomalies occur in education with *Madame le professeur* and *Madame le recteur* but other roles can be feminised (*inspectrice, directrice, proviseure, principale*).

The picture for Spanish is likewise somewhat complex since there is the *Real Academia Española*, which was founded in 1714 and updates its dictionary every decade. Twenty-two separate language academies had sprung up in the individual Latin American countries and there were efforts to create an international standard for that language. "The term *panhispanismo* was coined at the onset of the revolutionary movement in the soon-to-be-former colonies", Nadeau and Barlow explain in *The Story of Spanish* (2013: 357). Since 1951, there has been an association of *academias* from all the different Spanish-speaking countries, known by the acronym ASALE and based in Madrid.

It would be useful to explore the links between political stance and linguistic purism, although this falls outside the scope of the present book. However, it is interesting to note that the rise of Mussolini in Italy in the 1930–1940s led to an interesting development in the language of sport. Although Harpastum (or Hap-rustum), also referred to as the small ball game, was a popular ball game played in the Roman Empire (www.topendsports.com/sport/extinct/harpastum.htm, last accessed on 13.01.21) many people claim that football was introduced to Italy by the English in the 19th century and until then, Italians had happily used English terminology. The Fascists were concerned to preserve the purity of the Italian language, however, and so they introduced Italian terms such as *rete* (goal), *calcio di rigore* (penalty), *fuorigioco* (offside) and *calcio d'angolo* (corner) (www.europassitalian. com/learn/history/, accessed on 13.01.21. See also www.theguardian.com/travel/ 2009/jul/15/learn-italian-phrases-football, accessed on 13.01.21 for more Italian football terminology).

In a similar vein, the National Socialists introduced the term *entartete Kunst* or 'degenerate art' in Germany to describe many of the works produced during the Weimar Republic by painters such as the German Expressionists Max Ernst and Paul Klee. Another well-known example of the manipulation of language through deliberate alteration of meaning can be seen in George Orwell's *Animal Farm*, where the ruling pigs adapt the wording of the 'seven commandments', created by all the animals, to suit their own purposes and achieve supremacy over the other animals.

Writing in 2009, Doris Steffens described some of the lexical changes she had observed in German in the 20 years since the fall of the Berlin Wall in 1989 (*20 Jahre Mauerfall – Zur Wortschatzentwicklung seit der Wendezeit* https://core.ac.uk/ download/pdf/83653613.pdf, accessed on 13.01.21). Many of the expressions used in the former GDR became obsolete after German Union in October 1990, she explained, and inhabitants of the new German states were quick to adopt terms used by the majority rather than using words that had been widely used for the past 40 years. Other factors such as the growth of globalisation also impacted on the German language. Some of the new words that entered the language around 1990 turned out to be short-lived (e.g. *Zukunftsminister* – Minister for the Future, a post that no longer exists). Steffens also mentions that a number of neologisms were anticipated in German following the terrorist attacks of September 11, 2001, but only one made its mark on the language, *Antiterrorkrieg* (war on terror).

It is worth bearing in mind that the norms for inclusivity in standard language tend to vary from culture to culture. In a recent editing assignment, one of the authors noticed that, even in the social sciences, some Francophone writers were less aware of the need to use gender-inclusive language, such as the pronoun 'they' for instance, than were their British counterparts.

There are many changes in the way we now process language in certain areas currently considered sensitive, causing us to rethink attitudes and values that seemed well established not so long ago. Take, for example, attitudes to sex: a significant change to our attitudes and values in the West occurred back in the Sixties, when a more 'permissive society' started to emerge. The Second World War had already had an enormous impact on sex and morals, where the uncertainty of the future led many people to adopt a *carpe diem* attitude towards sex. The Cambridge dictionary defines a permissive society as "the type of society that has existed in most of Europe, Australia and North America since the 1960s, in which there is a great amount of freedom of behaviour, especially sexual freedom" (http s://dictionary.cambridge.org/dictionary/english/permissive-society). The term translates easily in the Romance languages to: *société permissive* (Fr); *società permissiva* (It); *sociedad permisiva* (Sp); and in German to *permissive Gesellschaft*. Attitudes to homosexuality had changed little since the end of WWII, as in the sad case of Alan Turing – one of the greatest cryptanalysts and mathematicians of the 20th century and a victim of homophobia. The prevailing moral attitudes of the time and the laws in force were highly discriminatory, as was the language used to describe homosexuality. While some progress was made on gay rights from the 1960s, it would be decades before sexual diversity became widely accepted in the West and attitudes to gender began to change significantly.

Elsewhere, change is also afoot: "It's all ova for Czech women's suffix" is the title of an article by Tim Gosling in *The Times* (9 July 2021), who reports that "Czech feminists are celebrating a victory against the patriarchy after a bill was passed ending the legal requirement to add the suffix 'ova' to women's names". It will take effect in January 2022. The writer comments that it was approved "despite claims that the change threatens grammatical, and even social chaos". He adds that campaigners claimed the requirement was "archaic and demeaning" because historically the ending 'ova' was the possessive form of the surname of a father or husband. But as David Hutt points out in Euronews (16 June 2021), the change is controversial:

> For many linguists, taking away the gendered suffix of a surname will greatly complicate the intricate system of declension and grammar in the Czech

language, in which the various suffixes attached to nouns, adjectives and verbs are essential in differentiating people in sentences.

In recent times, another important development has occurred in the way we frame gender, with a move away from using binary gender (male and female) to referencing in a more neutral manner. In the 20th century, many women would have been quite happy to be classed as an *actress* or an *air hostess/stewardess*, considering these terms normal and dignified. However, references to these professions in English have been largely supplanted respectively by the non-binary forms *actor* and *flight attendant*. But, as an article in *The New Indian Express – Edex* points out, "non-sexist language has not become popular in countries where English is spoken either as a second or foreign language". The writer, Albert P. Rayan, mentions that in India thinking tends to be stereotyped, with the word *doctor* implying a male and *nurse* a female. On the issue of gender-neutral language (GNL), he suggests using *themself* (instead of *himself* and *herself*), which he indicates as widely used in contemporary English (www.edexlive.com/op inion/2018/sep/07/why-its-important-to-use-gender-neutral-language-3877.html).

Writing in an autobiographical work published in 2018, the author of fantasy literature Ursula Le Guin provocatively remarked on gender issues that:

> I am a man. Now you may think I've made some kind of silly mistake about gender, or maybe that I'm trying to fool you, because my first name ends in -a … I'm a man, and I want you to believe and accept this as a fact, just as I did for many years. … Women are a very recent invention. … When I was born, there actually were only men. People were men. They all had one pronoun, his pronoun; so that's who I am. I am the generic me.
>
> *(Ursula Le Guin 2018: 235)*

What Le Guin is highlighting is that sexism is (still) inbuilt in language and reflected in all walks of life. An article by Mark Peters for the BBC points out that

> Disentangling language and gender isn't easy, since the two have a long-term relationship that is complicated. The two intermingle in so many ways, some obvious and some more subtle. Neanderthalic behaviour such as calling a woman 'honey' or 'baby' is as out of fashion as cave paintings. Particularly in the workplace, certain kinds of sexist language are simply no longer accepted. But there's mounting evidence, anecdotal and scientific, that gender-propelled language and attitudes are still common in many places of employment. Gendered words are thrown around constantly. In performance reviews, women tend to receive feedback that's vague ('you had a great year' for example) or sexist, such as a disproportionate number of comments on communication style, while men get clearer feedback about specific skills related to actual job performance. The disparity in how men and women are addressed can be even worse in emails.
>
> *(In "The hidden sexism in workplace language", 30 March 2017: www.bbc.com/ worklife/article/20170329-the-hidden-sexism-in-workplace-language)*

The traditional dominance of the masculine gender in Romance languages is discussed in an interesting article which appeared on the website Global Voices ("Are Romance languages becoming more gender neutral?" 11 September 2020; https://globalvoices.org/2020/09/11/are-romance-languages-becoming-more-gender-neutral). Collaborators with mother tongues in various Romance languages discuss how GNL is being addressed:

> Activism for gender neutrality in language is part of a larger movement to question, resist, and dismantle sexism conveyed through language. Activists claim that the dominance of the masculine gender in languages is not neutral, as purported, but rather has been imposed historically through ideological and political processes.

In French, for example,

> the first way of adopting inclusive writing is to use existing neutral forms where possible, for example, *le lectorat* (the readership) instead of *les lecteurs* (m.) or *les lectrices* (f.). The second technique explicitly includes both masculine and feminine endings. For example, the 'e' and 'ice' endings, often used for feminine forms, would follow the masculine form, for example, *lecteur·ice·s* (readers). However, only a year later we learn that France's education ministry has banned the use of gender-inclusive words in classrooms, saying they 'harm' learning. The edict highlighted the practice of introducing full stops in the middle of words to signal both masculine and feminine endings. An example would be changing *amis* into *ami.e.s*.
>
> (Clinton 2021)

Indeed, whilst the French administrative authorities claim that they are sensitive to the need for gender equality, they remain anxious to uphold the rules of grammar and syntax. The latter concern means that there is serious scepticism about "le recours à l'écriture dite « inclusive »" (having recourse to so-called 'inclusive writing'). In its official bulletin of 5 May 2021 The French Department of Education, for instance, produced recommendations entitled *Règles de féminisation dans les actes administratifs du ministère de l'Éducation nationale, de la Jeunesse et des Sports et les pratiques d'enseignement* (www.education.gouv.fr/bo/21/Hebdo18/MENB2114203C.htm).

The Spanish example in the Global Voices article reports that

> Several attempts at gender neutrality have been implemented over the past decades in Spanish; the earliest included the use of 'x' and '@' to replace the vowel that marks gender such as *'tod@s'* ('everyone'). More recently, activists started using the 'e' as a generic neutral alternative, and the neuter pronoun 'elle' emerged as an alternative for 'él/ella' ('he/she').

(Portuguese, Catalan and Romanian are also discussed in this article, with Romanian apparently lagging behind the moves towards inclusivity in other languages in this group.)

In fact, Romanian does have a neuter gender, which mainly refers to objects, but interestingly it is masculine in the singular form and feminine in the plural (ambigeneric).

In Germany, the *Gesellschaft für deutsche Sprache* (GfdS), a politically independent association working to uphold and research the German language, is critical of the widely used *Gendersternchen* (gender asterisk) on the grounds that it conforms neither with the rules of German grammar nor spelling. This society supports the idea of non-discriminatory language but does not consider the *Gendersternchen* as an appropriate linguistic tool to implement this since it could result in ungrammatical forms such as *Ärzt*in, Bauer*in* or *Kolleg*in*. A German website dedicated to linguistic issues related to gender awareness www.genderleicht.de/Textlabor/genderstern-nach-umlaut/ suggests that such infelicities can be avoided by repeating the word in full, with an asterisk between the two versions, namely *Bauern*Bäuerinnen* or *Franzosen*Französinnen*, rather than adopting a slash between the two words in each case, which is the solution proposed by Duden. It was reported by Bernward Loheide in *Geo Magazin* on 16 February 2021 that the German dictionary Duden had done away with the generic masculine so that the word *Mieter*, meaning a *tenant*, is now defined as a *männliche Person, die etwas gemietet hat* (male person who has rented something) and for inclusivity *Mieterinnen und Mieter* or new forms with the asterisk *Mieter*innen* and underscore *Mieter_innen* are used (www.geo.de/wissen/24003-rtkl-sprachpolitik-ein-mieter-ist-maennlich-der-duden-streicht-das-generische).

In response to widespread media coverage of the gender inclusivity and gender neutrality debate in Germany and many other countries, the ITI German network held an extremely informative webinar on gender-inclusive language on 29 May 2021. Dr Emily Spiers and Sascha Stollhans from the Department of Languages and Cultures at Lancaster University highlighted some of the recent developments that may affect the working practices of translators, particularly those working into languages that are grammatically gendered, such as German (https://politico.eu/a rticle/debate-over-gender-inclusive-neutral-language-divides-Germany, accessed on 02.06.21). They explained that the United Nations aims to provide resources enabling staff to communicate in a gender-inclusive way in all six of its official languages (see www.un.org/en/gender-inclusive-language). Meanwhile, rather than waiting for language to evolve organically, people have started thinking creatively about language in efforts to eliminate binary gender bias. Gender-neutral and non-binary pronouns along similar lines to English *they* (as a singular pronoun, the use of which dates back to Shakespearean times) have now been proposed in many languages, they said. In Swedish, for instance, the non-binary pronoun *hen* was created at the instigation of the LGBT movement, and in German, Anna Heger has been working on a whole declension table for the non-binary pronoun *xier* (www.annaheger.de/pronouns). There is no intention for such systems to be prescriptive, merely for people to accept them when others use them. In order to cover all translators, teachers, and students, gender-fair terms derived from the present participles of verbs are now being used, namely *die Übersetzenden, die Lehrenden* and *die Studierenden*. In spoken language, German newsreaders use a pause or a glottal stop to account for a gender asterisk or colon in a text.

Further developments in German-speaking countries were featured in various website articles in June 2021 (www.politico.eu/article/germany-gender-neutral-language-news/?utm_medium=Social&utm_source=Twitter#Echobox=1624302275).

Political correctness is increasingly important for interpreters. Kirsty Heimerl-Moggan, an interpreter working in this language pair, said there was a lot more terminology than when she started out, adding, "gender-related terminology for example is quite a minefield with many different terms to choose between and new terms constantly being added".

Dr Brigitte Scott, a translator and editor, who now lives in Austria after working in the UK for many years, said

> You have to pay more attention to inclusive language (gender-sensitive, ethnicity-sensitive). With so much research being published in English by non-native authors, meanings of words are creeping in that differ from standard British English. This I hear is also true of the English spoken in the corridors in Brussels among EU officials and their entourage.

PAUSE FOR THOUGHT 6

1. If you translate from English into a target language that uses masculine and feminine forms for professions (such as the gender-neutral *flight attendant*), do you feel that you are using sexist language?

2a. As a translator or interpreter, would you find it helpful to make a list of culturally insensitive vocabulary in both your source language/s and target language to ensure you do not use it in your work inadvertently?

2b. If you were asked to translate emails or Twitter comments containing offensive language as a professional job (say, for a criminal lawyer or a court) would you refuse the job or accept it?

Group work: Discuss the implications of 2b and more generally of dealing with insensitive language as a translator or interpreter.

New ideas and changes in the social order can affect language, even though the impact may only be temporary. For instance, the French revolutionaries introduced a new calendar, with new names for the months, starting with *Vendémiaire*, which was derived from *vendange* (grape harvest) and fell in the autumn quarter. Most of these new names are now long forgotten but vestiges of them survive in French. The second month in the Republican calendar was *Brumaire*, aptly named after the fogs that appear at this time of the year. It gained fame in history books following the coup d'état of 18 Brumaire in the year VIII (9 November 1799), when Napoleon overthrew the government of the Directory and replaced it with the Consulate. *Thermidor*, the eleventh month in the Republican calendar was preserved for posterity by a roundabout route when a Paris chef created a gourmet treat to celebrate the opening of a play of the same name. The play may not have stood the test of time but the lobster dish that the chef devised has perpetuated the name *Thermidor*. For a glossary of terms related to the French revolution, see www.translationdirectory.com/glossaries/glossary330.php and for a glossary of terms from the Russian revolution, see the British Library website www.bl.uk/russian-revolution/glossary.

The interaction of social change and language works in both directions: not only is language shaped by developments in society, it is also used as a tool to shape society or push it in a specific direction. Slogans coined by activists may well result in the success or failure of a campaign, while new trends and fashions bring an influx of new (or repurposed) words and phrases into a language, as was the case with the *Mariage pour tous* movement in France, which fought to make same-sex marriage legal there. The countermovement opposing equal marriage called itself by a similar name, *Manif pour tous*, and actually adopted many of the symbols and much of the pizzazz of Gay Rights parades. Interestingly, the 'brand' has now been adopted for other campaigns, with marchers protesting against the new French Bioethics Laws at the National Assembly in Paris on 27 July 2020 under the *Manif pour tous* banner (https://francais.rt.com/france/77206-rassemblement-manif-pour-tous-devant-assemblee-nationale-contre-projet-loi-bioethique; accessed on 26.08.20). As a translator, you need to ensure that you know what you are dealing with: the adoption by activists of strategies of this kind could be very confusing so it is important to check the facts in various sources from different ends of the political spectrum so you can detect any hidden agendas.

On the wider agenda of LGBTQ+ we learn that "A literary sensation in the Netherlands, *The Discomfort of Evening* is the debut novel by [Marieke Lucas] Rijneveld, 29, a non-binary author whose preferred pronouns are *they* or *them*" (Sherwin 2020). It is worth pointing out that **they** has another function, as well as indicating the third person plural of *him/her/it*. It has long been an effective device for expressing impersonality, which English does not 'do' as well as many other languages (French with *on* and German with *man* for instance). However, using *they* for a singular reference can easily cause **ambiguity**. An equity release company that advertises on TV initially preferred to use *they* in the following utterance, when explaining to potential interested viewers when and how any money raised through the scheme would be repaid: "They do not have to repay the money until they have passed away or gone into long-term care" (Age Partnership). In a strenuous effort to avoid using 'you' (presumably considered insensitive as linked to the euphemistic 'passed away'), the copywriters used *they* to indicate both potential clients and family or heirs. Not content with one faux pas, a later version of the advert presented by a well-known TV figure, *does* use you (thus: *you* do not have to repay the money until *you* pass away), which is even more direct and referentially illogical. However, TV advertising relies on engaging viewers and impersonal forms create a barrier of remoteness, as in "Rather than having to make monthly repayments like a traditional loan, the money is paid back on death or if the borrower moves into care" (Anderson 2020). Somehow, while the written form may be considered to 'work', on television a greater level of informality (even where illogically and ungrammatically expressed) is considered preferable to remote impersonal language.

2.3 Environment and technology

Another source of new or repurposed language triggered by changing attitudes and values is the environment. Concerns about the influence of human action on the environment have been voiced for several decades, by lobby groups such as the WWF (World Wildlife Fund) and activists (e.g. on WWF's trawler *The Rainbow Warrior*; for more information on this ship, see http://emilyrussellhistoryinternal. weebly.com/the-rainbow-warrior.html). Other examples are the Extinction Rebellion movement and high-profile individuals, including world-famous naturalist David Attenborough and teenage activist Greta Thunberg. From saving rainforests to tackling climate change and global warming, from organic farming to attempts to disrupt the illegal trade in ivory and endangered species, we have become acutely aware of the environmental risks that future generations will face if we do not take urgent action. Interestingly, COVID-19 lockdowns globally reduced pollution levels as traffic levels declined and industries ceased operating and, forced to stay at home, people rediscovered cooking meals instead of buying fast food or eating out. In an article published in mid-August 2020 titled "Crop a load of this – How to get involved" we learn that:

> While the *nose-to-tail movement* advocates eating every part of an animal – *root-to-leaf eating* is all about making the most of the parts of vegetables we usually discard. A *plant-based restaurant* in Cambridge and London was among the first to use the leaves, tops and stalks of vegetables that are usually discarded, in all its dishes. To link with others to rescue farm produce and turn it into *value-added products* join Feedback's Gleaning Network, which works with UK farmers.
>
> *(Hargreaves 2020)*

What is interesting about the phrases in italics is the use of hyphenated noun compounds deployed adjectivally to describe emerging environmental trends like cutting food waste; at the same time, an earlier hyphenated form *value-added* is used.

One change that a group of farmers had called for was a decision by the European Parliament (ultimately unsuccessful) to ban labelling non-meat foods, such as bean burgers and vegan sausages, using names relating to meat products. The lobby group suggested that consumers could be confused if non-meat products were indicated using 'meat' names. Susie Dent points out that the Anglo-Saxon word *mete* originally referred to all kinds of food but that the meaning narrowed over time to refer only to animal flesh: "History tells us that language has always changed course according to the driving forces of culture, technology and taste. As always, our words will follow our lead". She cites the meat-based idiom *Es ist mir alles wurst* meaning 'I really don't care' or more literally 'It's all sausage to me' (in *One man's meat …*, *The i Newspaper*, 24–25 October 2020).

Another crucial environmental topic is climate change. Translators of science and technology texts need to read widely to develop an awareness of emerging research areas, such as the 'restoration ecology' technique that is being used to counteract the mass bleaching of corals. Technological change and innovations, such as deep learning neural networks, references to which we have seen feature regularly in patents in recent years, have now started to make their mark on machine translation. As a result, it is becoming increasingly sophisticated and more widely available, so that in order to find work, human translators need to expand their skill set to include post-editing and other activities that as yet remain beyond the competence of artificial intelligence or robots. Some such systems are currently unable to draw a distinction between alternative dictionary renderings, such as *thanksgiving* and *acknowledgements* for the German term *Danksagung,* and the contexts in which they are appropriate, which is why post-editing remains in demand. (See Chapter 5 for recommended reading in this field, both existing and ongoing.)

Sociocultural change also implies **technological change**, one of the consequences of which is the gradual demise of the legacy or traditional (i.e. old) media, which could well affect translators and their workflow. Over the course of our careers in translation, we have seen huge developments in the tools available to translators, progressing from Dictaphones (dictating machines that recorded your voice on a large floppy disc the size of a long-playing record) to dongles and from telex machines that used ticker tape to machine translation and computer-assisted translation (CAT) tools. Translators working in patents and intellectual property have always needed to be aware of new technological and scientific developments because, in order for a patent application to be granted, the concept underlying the invention has to demonstrate three things: novelty, an inventive step and industrial applicability (which means that it has to be useful). In other words, to satisfy these criteria, something has to have changed in the design of the product, process or device that makes it stand apart from existing inventions. (www.wipo.int/edocs/m docs/aspac/en/wipo_ip_cmb_17/wipo_ip_cmb_17_3.pdf).

Another recent technological breakthrough that might eventually be of benefit to sci-tech and patent translators, and to anyone working from home who needs to keep confidential work secure online, has been achieved by quantum physicists at the University of Bristol. By using a new technique based on the spooky phenomenon of entanglement, a phenomenon in which the quantum states of two or more objects have to be described with reference to each other, even though the individual objects may be spatially separated, Dr Siddarth Joshi and his team have brought the concept of a quantum internet one step closer (see Joshi 2020). In https://sciencex.com/news/

2020-09-quantum-internet-breakthrough-malicious-hacking.html, Dr Joshi explains that "Quantum communication creates keys using individual particles of light (photons), which – according to the principles of quantum physics – are impossible to make an exact copy of" (see also: www.sciencedaily.com/terms/quantum_enta nglement.htm, accessed on 18.09.20).

As technology advanced, the use of 'textspeak' and emoticons became more widespread and, according to Lauren Collister, a sociolinguist at the University of Pittsburgh, such phenomena helped to streamline English and update it for the 21st century (www.wpr.org/defense-textspeak-socio-linguist-says-emojis-and-lols-are-m odernizing-english, accessed on 07.09.20). This article by Scottie Lee Meyers and Erik Lorenzsonn explains that the punctuation-based symbols first introduced in 1982 by Scott Fahlman, a Carnegie Mellon professor, have become commonly used as what linguists call 'discourse markers'.

3 Language variation and change

Recent or past, gradual or abrupt, social and cultural changes have an impact on the development and evolution of language. Whether we are aware of change or not, the society we live in and the language we speak are continually evolving. In *Fundamentals of Translation*, Sonia Colina makes a distinction between **language variation** and **language change** (where *variation* reflects differences in the way a language is used from one context to another): "Unlike variation, language change is very difficult to observe, especially for an individual" she writes, suggesting that it may only be noticeable across generations (Colina 2015: 183). We might assume that it is contact between languages that causes changes, but according to James Milroy, an expert in sociolinguistics, "Linguistic change is initiated by speakers, not by languages", suggesting that linguistic change is an internal, rather than external, dynamic (Milford 2020: 84). Essentially, variations in the day-to-day language of a community derive mainly from the spoken language, therefore many lexical and grammatical changes that become established derive, as Colina points out, from "oral, informal and generally less prestigious varieties, where variation is more common because of the nature of the oral medium" (Colina, *ibid:* 184). This also explains why linguistic changes, whether new forms or those borrowed from other languages, are often considered to be 'corrupt' forms of the established norms of a language, and which therefore debase the language.

The area of linguistics most relevant to the theme of this book is **sociolinguistics**, a discipline which considers a piece of language (or discourse) in a social setting where the different contexts inform the type of language used. As Peter Stockwell (2007) points out in a book written to explain sociolinguistics to students: "There are two types of variables in sociolinguistics: the **social variable** that determines a variation in language (such as gender, geography, age, occupation) and the **linguistic variable** (a language, **dialect**, style, register, syntactic pattern, or particular sound)". While our book does not focus specifically on sociolinguistics, we refer to and apply concepts from this area of linguistics where relevant to underpin the analysis we present.

In sociolinguistics, the term **language variation** refers to an intermediate or transitional lexical or morphological stage before the final acceptance of the word, phrase or spelling in the host language as an established form (e.g. *to-day* > *today*). Once the new or altered form becomes widespread and is in everyday use, a language change can be said to have taken place. But variation is not only lexical or orthographic: in everyday speech once-formal boundaries of language may be stretched, as exemplified by the following announcement of a train driver nearing a London station: "Hello ladies and gentlemen. In a few minutes we will be arriving at Kings Cross. Passengers are reminded to take all your belongings with you". The driver shows some familiarity with an impersonal official register, but from the start swings between informal and formal language in an attempt to make the announcement impersonal (with *Hello*, followed by the formal mode of address *ladies and gentlemen*). The driver appears oblivious to the changes between first, second and third person; what is important is to press home the message so that passengers do not leave any possessions on the train. The travelling public may well not notice the mixed formal/informal register of the greeting and information, or the confusion between the third person plural *Passengers* followed by the second person possessive adjective and pronoun, but they will no doubt get the gist of the message (if they are listening). In sociolinguistic terms, what the driver is doing can be termed **code-switching** (i.e. moving from one social context to another). This example of the train driver's mixed-code discourse shows only too clearly that English is a language that can easily 'bend the rules', particularly in speech, combining **informality** and **formality** in a single utterance. The 'elasticity' of mixed registers in English is frequently difficult to translate or interpret: most languages have more complex grammatical systems than English, as well as different **politeness** codes, therefore jumping from one register to another is far less feasible.

In an article in the *ITI Bulletin* on "Terms of Endearment" (Jul–Aug 2018), Susan Bassnett makes an interesting point about differing systems of politeness and affection across languages. On a flight from Italy to Germany the pilot addressed the passengers in English as 'Dear Guests', which might sound curious to an English speaker. She suggests that "The use of 'dear', which is presumably a translation of *Liebe* (sic) is interesting, because it signals almost a kind of intimacy", in a similar fashion to the train driver's attempt to water down the formality of standard communication norms with passengers. To us, it sounds rather like the style you would find in a welcome leaflet provided in a hotel room.

PAUSE FOR THOUGHT 7

If you were *translating* what the train driver said in the example above in a literary context, such as a novel, how would you proceed? Would you attempt to make your target language reflect these idiosyncrasies (risking confusion and accusations of bad grammar) or opt for an informal or formal register? If the former, how colloquial would you make the language, and why? If you were *interpreting* the driver, would your approach differ? If so, how?

> These 'dilemmas' reveal the real choices that translators and interpreters face every day. The example above underlines the connection (or disconnect) between the social aspect of communication and the tenets of 'correct' language use.

As we have seen during the COVID-19 pandemic, words and phrases typical of the language and register of experts, such as the health professionals thrust blinking into the limelight, can be rapidly absorbed in contemporary discourse. Take the expression **herd immunity**, defined by the Bloomberg School of Public Health at Johns Hopkins University: "When most of a population is immune to an infectious disease, *herd immunity* provides indirect protection (also called *herd protection*) to those who are not immune to the disease" (https://www.jhsph.edu/covid-19/articles/a chieving-herd-immunity-with-covid19.html). Before COVID-19, people with little knowledge of the biological sciences or medicine might have associated 'herd immunity' with farming and animal husbandry, even though the concept was discussed in a medical paper back in 1923 (Topley & Wilson 1923). However, specialist vocabulary and register from different fields can be swiftly deployed by the media to keep the general public up-to-date as events unfold, at a time when it is crucial to ensure that instructions are followed. To be effective, this specialist language needs to be communicated in conjunction with explanations and definitions.

Public perceptions of words and phrases suddenly in the glare of publicity, like *herd immunity*, tend to fall in and out of favour as situations evolve. In the early stages of the coronavirus pandemic, herd immunity initially seemed to be a desirable goal, but when very high numbers of people started to fall sick with a severe form of the illness, resulting in many deaths, public opinion changed; when vaccination became widely available, herd immunity seemed once again to be a logical stance in terms of keeping the virus at bay, given the ability of COVID-19 to mutate with relative ease. Or perhaps it was simply a recognition that this virus will probably always be with us, and the only way forward is to create as much immunity as possible in the population.

The 'fast-track' entry of specialist terms in everyday use is triggered by emergencies and fast-moving scenarios (for example, terrorist attacks or natural disasters) which affect large numbers of people. Information can be disseminated so rapidly nowadays it is not surprising that concepts once unfamiliar to us are suddenly heard in everyday speech, used by people who would not normally refer to 'herd immunity', 'social distancing', 'quarantine', 'confinement', 'anosmia' (the loss of the sense of smell), 'variant', 'surge testing' and 'vaccine hesitancy'. The uptake of specialist lexis into colloquial discourse patterns creates a mixed code (almost a 'bluffer's guide', which speakers use to show (off) their ability to deploy specialist 'labels').

3.1 Formal or informal register

Variations in language from one setting to another depend on who is talking, who they are talking to and what they are talking about. For example, someone speaking to a friend in an informal social setting may well use a lower register (or level of language) than when communicating with someone in an official capacity. Variation is often a question of status: most people can adapt and vary the level of language they use to suit the situation, as we have seen in the example in the previous paragraph. In English, moving between **social registers** may appear relatively straightforward: the second person form of address – *you* – can be communicated informally or formally (but as the equity release advert example shows only too well, such 'impersonal' use can cause serious problems of logic if not handled carefully). Addressing someone by their first name is another way of indicating informality, yet first names can also be used between people who do not know each other, as a way of rendering communication less daunting (for example, in a doctor–patient, salesperson–customer or employer–employee relationship where the setting may indicate a formal relationship). According to Jodi Glickman's article in the *Harvard Business Review* on November 1, 2011, "Addressing people by their first name is now the norm in corporate America (though not in the rest of the world — to the ongoing consternation of business travelers)" (https:// hbr.org/2011/11/the-power-of-a-first-name, accessed on 26.08.20). Finally, the use of titles (with or without a surname) usually signals a degree of formality, where the perceived social status may be the same between the speakers (creating a level playing field) or where one person is showing politeness and/ or respect for the other speaker. Interpreter Kirsty Hemmerl-Moggan believes that informality has not increased with her business clients. In works councils in Europe delegates always did use the less formal *du* with each other but *Sie* with managers and they still do. What she has noticed is that mild swearing such as calling a situation 'ein richtiger Sch-' are more common than they were when she was a child.

English into French translator Philippe Galinier alerted us to a trend in French towards some increased informality and imports from US English, leading to a gap between what the guardians of the French language, such as the Académie Française, prescribe and what French speakers actually say. For instance, most people say le Covid, whereas the French Academy insists that it should be la Covid, because it's la maladie, as Kim Willshire points out in www.theguardian.com/world/2020/may/13/le-la-covid-coronavirus-acronym-feminine-academie-francaise-france. Philippe added,

> While it is true that in some industries like IT, cybersecurity, management, etc. there is a profusion of "trendy" English words, it is refreshing to note that when it comes to the new French words used in connection with the Covid pandemic the language of Molière appears to be holding its own.

He quoted a French linguist who explained that the French scientific community, public bodies and media have been using French words to talk about the pandemic with the exception of the odd English term ('cluster' instead of foyer épidémique). New COVID-19 words had been coined following a rather natural pattern; for example, by adding prefixes, which is typical of how French words are created:

thus 'confinement' (lockdown), then 'déconfinement' (coming out of lockdown), and even 'reconfinement' (second or new lockdown).

On 5 June 2020, Genie Godula talked on France 24 about some of the new buzz-words coined during the pandemic (www.france24.com/en/france/20200605-french-connections-la-covid-19-how-coronavirus-has-affected-the-french-language), such as *les gestes barrière*, a term used to describe actions to achieve social distancing, *le skypéro* (consumption of an apéritif with friends on Skype) and *l'apérue* (the apéro consumed on the street during *le déconfinement*). More French pandemic-related neologisms are listed in an article by William Audureau entitled « *Lundimanche* », « *apérue* », « *coronabdos* » … *les nouveaux mots du confinement*, which appeared in *Le Monde* on 27 April 2020 (www.lemonde.fr/m-perso/article/2020/04/27/lundimanche-aperue-coronabdos-les-nouveaux-mots-du-confinement_6037915_4497916.html).

Philippe has also observed a tendency in French journalistic writing to create new metaphors, such as *emboliser*, which has the literal sense of 'to cause an embolism', that is, to create a blockage, as in this headline from France Info about a crisis in which French hospitals were overstretched, even two years before the pandemic. "'Là, nous sommes vraiment embolisés" : aux urgences, usagers et professionnels de santé tirent la sonnette d'alarme' (France Info online, 19 March 2018).

Kari Koonin FITI, who translates from Afrikaans, Dutch and German into English told us: "I have noticed a distinct trend towards incomplete **sentences**, i.e. sentences without a main verb, particularly in Dutch but also, recently, and surprisingly, in German too". She added that, when she joined the profession some 30 years ago, writers producing material in German paid far more attention to grammar and style than people do nowadays. She added that there is less formality than there used to be: "Over the years I have noticed the ever more widespread use of the familiar form of address in Dutch and increasingly in German too – that would have been unheard of between people who have never met, a decade or so ago".

Emma Gledhill FITI, a translator based in Switzerland, told us that the use of messaging services and social media has led to a vast amount of information being circulated, resulting in a blurring of the boundaries between written and spoken language, particularly in those media.

Older generations are often critical of directions that society – but also language – takes. This **conservative prescriptivism** (or linguistic prescription) is described in *Introducing Linguistics* (2012) as

> a powerful force in society, especially one with written traditions. Educated people … have acquired a command of the standard language of their day, especially the written standard, and they are often people reluctant to accept any changes into the language they have grown up with and learned in school.
>
> *(Trask & Mayblin 2012)*

Therefore, it is no wonder that many British people point the finger at the creeping Americanisation of (British) English, regardless of the fact that some of the lexis that purists object to originated in Britain, took root in the USA then found its way back home: for example, *I guess* and *gotten*. In an article on the penetration of Americanisms in British English, Hephzibah Anderson makes the point that we can no longer tell which words are 'Americanisms' and which are not, as they have become so entrenched in our everyday language. She suggests that language seems to operate on a 'one-in one-out' basis, giving the example of 'awesome' having largely displaced 'marvellous'. She concludes that "It might seem tactless to bemoan the state of any branch of all-conquering English when so many other languages are being wiped out entirely. But ultimately, the battle isn't really one of British versus American English, but of individual experience versus the homo-genising effects of global digital culture" (Anderson 2017).

As time passes, people tend to forget that they themselves contributed to driving changes in society, culture and language when they were younger, by embracing new ideas, concepts and ways of expressing these through writing and speech. The new is as seductive for the younger generations as it may be 'suspect' for more mature generations. Resistance to change is frequently a losing battle, as in the case of the letter 'z' replacing 's' in the *-ise* verb ending, though the change is not yet fully established in British English. We are still in a transitional phase (as happened with *to-day* and *to-morrow* which gradually joined forces in the 20th century to form single words) but increasingly in British English (probably driven by publishing) the *-ize* form seems to prevail. In much the same way, *any* and *more* have merged to form *anymore* (an Americanism that has now made its way into the Cambridge Dictionary!).

A publisher may be reluctant to use spelling that in many circles is considered rather 'old hat'. Science and technology writers, in particular, favour the *-ize* ending which is standard in literature in their areas of specialism. A seasoned translator may agonise over which form to use, being torn between the comfor-table standards of the past and the excitement of the new, but what might that decision depend on? Those who translate in domains where *-ize* is prevalent would no doubt conform to what is considered standard use. So, is the use of a form like *anymore* a question of principle, choice or the desire to conform to what is becoming the norm? Younger writers and translators are likely to (automatically) use more up-to-date words or spelling, reflecting current trends in language development.

Language change seems to be occurring more rapidly than it did in the past, when variations may have taken many years to consolidate into changes. Interest-ingly, *any longer* remains two words, presumably as it would look 'odd' as a single word. But *any longer* is now rather old-fashioned and losing currency against *any-more*, as it is simply 'longer'! Variation and change are driven not only by social factors (such as new trends and cultural borrowing), but also by practicality and aesthetic appeal.

Younger generations (and probably many adults) adopt and disseminate new forms, thus helping them to thrive; they may take root and 'edge out' an earlier form or forms or be relegated to the back burner. They may even reappear at a later date. For example, the adjective *cool*, which probably first appeared in the

Thirties, lay largely dormant in much the same way as a dormouse in the latter part of the 20th century, only to reappear with the same **meaning** in the 21st century. It can be found with its modern meaning in a short story by the African-American writer Zora Neale Hurston in 1933, in her short story *The Gilded Six-Bits*, where she said of a male character: "And whut *(sic)* make it so cool, he got money 'cumulated. And womens give it all to 'im" (cited in https://slate.com/human-interest/2013/10/cool-the-etymology-and-history-of-the-concept-of-coolness.html, accessed on 26.08.20).

New slang words, phrases and abbreviations are appearing all the time, particularly in teen culture, driven by texting and social media. While slang terms might have spread to older generations in the past, eventually taking root more widely, juvenile slang nowadays across languages is often only understood by young people, despite the reach of the internet. An older translator asked to translate phone or text messages or blogs might have to think twice about accepting these jobs (unless they have a teenager they can consult!).

3.2 The internet as a driver of language change

The internet has had a tremendous impact on the divide between formal and informal language by making it far more fluid. Informal language is no longer confined to speech or quotations from spoken language but the open forum that is available to everyone online means that speech conventions are gradually being absorbed into written language. As the Canadian linguistics researcher Gretchen McCulloch points out in *Because Internet: Understanding how language is changing* (2020: 32), adolescence plays a key role in driving linguistic change within a society because "it's the last time that a whole population is entering a new social group all at once". She also attributes the fact that "the internet makes language change faster" to the huge increase in the number of 'weak ties' or interactions that you can have on applications such as Twitter with people you have never met or only know slightly. Such connections tend to lead to more linguistic change than the stronger ties that exist in a close-knit society such as Iceland (*ibid:* 36).

PAUSE FOR THOUGHT 8

Imagine you are a middle-aged or elderly 'Brit' writing an article for publication or translating one. Would you insist on the printers using the *-ise* spelling? Or, as a younger person, would you automatically use the *-ize* ending?

It is part of our professional development as translators or interpreters to update our knowledge of both our source and target language/s in much the same way as we need to read widely to develop our knowledge of new events, concepts and vocabulary. Sonia Colina (*ibid:* 215) stresses the importance of keeping up-to-date with language when discussing social aspects of translation, commenting: "Translators, as language professionals, need to understand how language variation and change operate and affect language, so that their translation practices and decisions are not based on personal biases and lay views about language, but, rather, on a principled understanding of how language interacts with society". An awareness of change, whether in society, culture, science or technology triggered by events, new research or cultural initiatives, is therefore crucial to the ability of linguists to work effectively and confidently. Anyone who has lived abroad and translated or interpreted as an 'expat' will know how easy it is to lose touch with reality, despite the presence of the internet, social media, and so on. The 'freshness' of the mother tongue has an annoying and unobtrusive habit of slipping away, which sometimes only becomes apparent on returning permanently to the home country.

Coming back to Britain after many years abroad, before the advent of the internet, one of the authors suffered from what she termed 'Rip Van Winkle syndrome', where she found that the English language had moved on in the 20 years she had lived abroad and despite having returned for frequent holidays, she felt like an outsider. (In the story of the same name by the American author Washington Irving, Rip Van Winkle falls asleep having imbibed liquor offered to him by dwarves, only to wake up 20 years later, where time has passed and he has grown to be an old man.) This story clearly shows how language is a communal and social phenomenon, and where meaning is constructed and interpreted in context. In extreme cases, a 'wild child' (or feral child) who has lived isolated from other human beings, experiences great difficulty in human language acquisition.

It is not only translators who are affected by social and linguistic change. Interpreters too have been forced to adapt their professional working patterns as a result of the COVID-19 pandemic. In the July–August 2020 issue of *ITI Bulletin*, five interpreters revealed how they had readjusted to remote video and telephone working practices, using Microsoft Teams and the Zoom interpreting platform, and Remote Simultaneous Interpreting (or RSI; *Distanced Voices*, pp. 16–17). Our own findings from interviews with interpreters are presented in Chapter 5.

3.3 Changes in spoken language

As for the trends in language change that interpreters might need to be aware of, a blog post entitled *English Accents – Estuary* by James Myatt, which appeared online at www.word-connection.fr on 31 August 2020, claimed that Estuary (which he defines as the accent of north Kent and southern Essex, adopted by the comedian Ricky Gervais, actor Russell Brand and chef Jamie Oliver) may replace received pronunciation as standard English within the next 50 years. The term appears to have originated in October 1984 with an article in the *Times Educational Supplement* by UK linguist David Rosewarne, who wrote:

> Estuary English is a variety of modified regional speech. It is a mixture of non-regional and local south-eastern English pronunciation and intonation. If one imagines a continuum with RP and London speech at either end, 'Estuary English' speakers are to be found grouped in the middle ground. The

heartland of this variety lies by the banks of the Thames and its estuary, but it seems to be the most influential accent in the south-east of England. It is to be heard on the front and back benches of the House of Commons and is used by some members of the Lords, whether life or hereditary peers. It is well established in the City, business circles, the Civil Service, local government, the media, advertising as well as the medical and teaching professions in the south-east. 'Estuary English' is in a strong position to exert influence on the pronunciation of the future.

It appears to be a continuation of the long process by which London pronunciation has made itself felt. This started in the later Middle Ages when the speech of the capital started to influence the Court and from there changed the Received Pronunciation of the day.

In 1998, Britons were shocked by such a deviation from standard UK pronunciation when Tony Blair was heard code-switching on a popular television talk show hosted by Des O'Connor. This even came to the attention of a US journalist, Sarah Lyall, who commented on it in the *New York Times* on 18 June, claiming that the then Prime Minister had said "They pu' on a li'l show for us". And referring to a horse he had been given in a French village he had dropped an aitch saying, "'e's come back to England" (Lyall 1998).

The glottal stop, often detected when Londoners only partly sound the letter 't' is a typical feature of the modern accent in and around the capital. It is defined in Oxford Dictionaries as "a consonant formed by the audible release of the airstream after complete closure of the glottis. It is widespread in some non-standard English accents and in some other languages, such as Arabic, it is a standard consonant" (https://languages.oup.com/google-dictionary-en, accessed on 08.09.20).

David Shariatmadari (2019: 86–87) outlines the 'communication accommodation theory' developed by the social psychologist Howard Giles, which postulates how we alter our speech when interacting with others, moving up or down the scale to either converge with or diverge from them. To illustrate Giles' theory, he quotes examples from 1960s pop music, which reflected sound features of US pronunciation, maintaining that Mick Jagger's singing voice, for instance, sounded very different from his southern-British speaking voice. A theory such as this could well explain how pronunciation has changed over time.

PAUSE FOR THOUGHT 9: AN EXERCISE DESIGNED IN
PARTICULAR FOR INTERPRETERS WITH ENGLISH AS THEIR L2

Watch one of the classic British films made in the 1940s or 50s, such as Noel Coward's 1945 movie *Brief Encounter* and listen carefully to the speech patterns and vowel sounds. Then watch a cookery programme made recently for UK television (such as Jamie Oliver's *Keep Cooking Family Favourites*) and/or an interview by a newscaster with members of the public and compare the language used in both. Do the characters in the celluloid classic all have similar accents or do you notice any variations? Can you identify any social or cultural factors that account for these differences? In the present-day broadcasts, can you spot any instances of Estuary English such as a glottal stop after the letter 't'? Listen for someone taking a breath after the consonant and before the next vowel. Is this something you should adopt or avoid?

In their preamble to a fascinating paper entitled *Language Development during Interstellar Travel*, two US linguistics experts, Andrew McKenzie, and Jeffrey Punske explain what happens when languages change. They say, "language change is more like a biological process than a fully predictable chemical one". And it happens quickly in smaller communities, as demonstrated by the phenomenon known as **'uptalk'**, the practice of ending a sentence on a rising note, which they claim, "has spread from small groups of young Americans and Australians to most of the English-speaking world".

These authors say that languages *diverge* mainly because "their speaking communities cease speaking to one another" and languages *converge* due to contact with other languages. A further factor in language change is 'language identity' with a language or dialect being used to show that its speakers belong within a specific community (http://people.ku.edu/~a326m085/LanguageDevelopmentInInterstellarTravel-0429.pdf).

Frances Parkes, a voice coach we interviewed for Chapter 5, mentioned her impression that the language used in interpreting in business contexts tends to be based on global English as a source language. Interpreters have seen big changes with their work regarding communication, she said. "In order to be heard at meetings, briefings and live reports, you have to be concise in your statements and answers to managers, in line with the bullet points of a presentation. A lot of people have struggled with this and use 'basically' and other fill in words such as 'you know'", she said. Her coaching had been designed to allow people to adjust to using key or active words, which is alien to some cultures in Africa and India, for instance. "However, young people have adapted well and [she believes] women are now more secure in the workplace and are learning more about the culture and politics of their workplace in line with men", she added.

Another trend prevalent in spoken English was highlighted in a BBC Radio 4 programme broadcast on 30 August 2020, presented by Lucrece Grehoua. Code-switching is a practice that is common in ethnically diverse communities and among young black professionals, where there are often social reasons for changing your accent as a function of the context and speakers have a wide linguistic repertoire.

4 Future changes

The internet is awash with predictions about future trends in health, education, business and lifestyle, which have proliferated since the start of the COVID-19 pandemic. Some of the changes forecast are already underway, galvanised by the pandemic; others are more subtle and concern the human side of business or globalization. Significantly, attitudes, behaviours and values feature strongly in predictions of future change: collaborative ways of working and communicating will continue to shape society through, for example, social media, cloud technology, work and life without borders. According to the organisation GHD, the idea of *social responsibility* in organisations will emerge more strongly, giving rise to *social capitalism* (social responsibility focused on the well-being of people; www.ghd.com/en/a bout-us/ten-emerging-trends-shaping-our-new-future.aspx). This people-centred focus is also reflected in education, through the concept of *liquid learning*. In a pre-COVID-19 article (2016), the authors describe liquid curricula as

> ones that focus on students' and tutors' stances and personal identities and provide opportunities to design modules and lessons in open and flexible ways. Universities need to stretch beyond open courseware and closed virtual learning environments. Instead learning would need to be created around a constellation of uncertainties, such as negotiated assessment, and open and flexible learning intentions.
>
> *(Steils et al. 2016)*

This is a prescient reference to the hybrid person-centred forms of teaching and learning and the linked technological and organisational mechanisms to deliver it that emerged due to the pandemic.

Many future changes will be driven by, and require, further developments in both technology and the upskilling and reskilling of human resources, particularly in remote working. Translators are well-placed for successful integration into new professional norms because most freelances already have well-established home offices and the peripatetic nature of the interpreting profession means that its practitioners are already adept at adapting to change, be it in location, social milieu or in the level of facilities provided. You will find further evidence of this in Chapter 5, where we present the views of various experienced language professionals on trends in the translation and interpreting sector and attempt to provide readers with a practice-centred overview of its inner workings.

PAUSE FOR THOUGHT 10

Before moving on to Chapter 2, use the internet to find terms such as those in italics in the section above that indicate new ways of working in different environments and check if there are standard translations of these terms in both your source and target languages. How would you proceed, as a translator or interpreter, if there are currently no standard equivalents?

2

EXPLORING LANGUAGE CHANGE AND THE IMPLICATIONS FOR TRANSLATION

In this chapter, we build on our discussion of the sociocultural and language changes described in Chapter 1 and assess their impact on language and translation, using texts from areas that show specific propensity for change: working life, science, technology, the environment, culture, politics and society.

Following the Overview, in Part 1 we discuss a selection of English texts using a Quick Identification Guide to source new and repurposed language, and in Part 2 we introduce a full Guidance Table for text analysis and show how this can be used in three translation comparisons: French, Italian and German into English.

1 Overview

In our contemporary society, unfolding events can have unforeseen and dramatic consequences. The repercussions of the coronavirus pandemic have affected virtually every aspect of our daily lives. While we cannot predict the future, the sociocultural changes it has left in its wake have generated a climate of uncertainty, with societies worldwide forced to adapt to changing circumstances. The terminology and phraseology connected with COVID-19 will persist as long as coronavirus continues to threaten public health, while new words and phrases will emerge in line with new research findings and sociocultural adaptations.

For example, the phrase *social distancing* (and its translated forms) is likely to become a fixture in most languages, in much the same way as *ground zero* became commonplace following the terrorist attack on the World Trade Center in New York in 2001. Phrases triggered by major events may 'spread their wings', settle in other contexts and become metaphors. *Lockdown* (widely used in connection with terror attacks) was already well established before the pandemic and has been repurposed from its original security function to indicate quarantine for health reasons. Some languages – for example Italian – use a 'parallel' lexical system, either

DOI: 10.4324/9781003136903-3

the English form or a coined phrase or **calque** in the mother tongue to convey new phrases: for example, in Italian *lockdown* is rendered *confinamento* and *social distancing* is *riduzione dei contatti* or *distanziamento sociale*; older words and phrases, originally used in a specific context, have become commonplace once more such as *quarantine* (from *quarantena*), used in a similar way to *lockdown*.

Romance languages, like French, tend to rely on calques (*distance sociale/distanciation sociale* and *confinement* for *social distancing*, though other forms are noted, such as *éloignement social* and *isolement social*). New acronyms emerge and established ones acquire new meanings – not so long ago, the English acronym PPE was universally familiar as Politics, Philosophy and Economics, rather than Personal Protective Equipment! Each 'repurposing' of a new word or phrase is a novel challenge for translators and heavily reliant on context. Every article or book, blog or advert shows new ways of adapting language to keep abreast of developments in all fields. It is interesting to note that some neologisms in the field of technology have emerged from the world of science fiction, a notable example being the concept of 'cyberspace', first invented by the science fiction writer William Gibson (according to Joshua Rothman in *The New Yorker*, 16 December 2019).

In the 28th edition of Duden, which appeared on 13 August 2020, the effects of the pandemic could already be seen with the addition of *Immunitätsnachweis*. Although the German Health Minister Jens Spahn's plan to introduce an immunity certificate giving exemption from certain regulations was soon dropped, it did make it into the dictionary (www.dw.com/de/der-duden-modernisiert-sich-und-mistet-a us/a-54559347). The latest fashion in men's hairstyles was also immortalised with the entry *Männerdutt*, which denotes the German version of the '*man bun*' and is used alongside the English term.

Every year, some of the major English language dictionaries choose a new word that has gained currency. For 2020, Oxford Dictionaries (OED), in a break with precedent, selected several new words or phrases that relate to the coronavirus pandemic but also other phenomena. However, not all these words are 'new': they are simply utterances in vogue and their currency will wax and wane as with previous 'new words'. An article on the BBC's website mentions that the OED's new words "are chosen to reflect 2020's ethos, mood, or preoccupations". They include *bushfires, COVID-19, WFH, lockdown, circuit-breaker, support bubbles, keyworkers, furlough, Black Lives Matter* and *moonshot*. As Amol Rajan points out in a continuation of the article, "It's inevitable that the pandemic should have rescued old words (*coronavirus*), super-charged some that were loitering in our culture (*furlough*), and – in the case of *COVID* – created a neologism. What's more striking to me is how the news cycle generates new phrases and usages" (www.bbc.co.uk/news/enterta inment-arts-55016543, 23.11.20). Rajan also mentions that references to Brexit have fallen by 80% over 2020. Despite the fact that the deadline for agreeing a deal with the EU was imminent, Brexit was no longer a 'hot topic' showing only too clearly how language change is increasingly driven by breaking news and by how people respond to emerging events.

Language change is certainly often due to some of the sociocultural factors mentioned in Chapter 1, but there are other influences too. In *Don't believe a Word* (2019: 34), linguistics expert David Shariatmadari explains that "changes in culture can result in changes in language" but he also mentions the process of 'reanalysis' (2019: 29) in which a word or phrase is reinterpreted at structural level. The examples he gives are *adder, apron* and *umpire*, all of which originally began with an 'n' preceding the initial vowel. Because these words often followed the indefinite article 'a', there would have been some ambiguity as to whether a speaker had said *a nadder* or *an adder*. Our own research indicates that in German, for instance, the initial 'n' has stayed put. A German referring to this poisonous snake will refer to *eine Natter*. This does not apply to the other two examples, which were derived from French, where they have now been replaced by *tablier* and *arbitre*.

Shariatmadari (*ibid*: 54–55) also explores the meanings of words, quoting Wittgenstein's insight into how we deploy them: "The meaning of a word is its use in the language" and he compares this view with what he calls "the etymological fallacy" (*ibid*: 44), a discredited theory according to which the "word's origin reveals you its true meaning", ignoring the fact that its meaning may have changed over time.

Another trend is the encroachment of English and indeed of *pseudo-anglicisms* into many other languages. In German, many English words have often evolved new meanings, for example *DJane* for a female disc jockey and *Handy* for a mobile phone as highlighted by Doris Steffens in a fascinating article published in Vol. 42, Issue 3 of *Sprachwissenschaft* (https://ids-pub.bsz-bw.de/frontdoor/deliver/index/docId/6433/file/Steffens_Von_Pseudoanglizismen_2017.pdf).

Dutch, too, is a victim of this trend. Kari Koonin FITI, who translates from Afrikaans, Dutch and German into English told us:

> The internet and the advent of TV streaming has had a huge impact on everyday speech in Dutch and German, with increasing use of (US) English interjections, words or phrases (especially swear words) and the influence of social media: *unfollowen* and *unfrienden*. You often hear "wow" and "yes" used by Dutch people in normal conversation. Also, verbs such as *streamen, influencen*, or *updaten* in Dutch, with the very complicated past participle *geüpdatet* which no-one can spell, plus webshop phrases and events like *Black Friday, Cyber Monday, New arrivals, Sale* and so on.

For a list of many more Dutch verbs modelled on English see https://onzetaal.nl/taaladvies/engelse-werkwoorden-met-een-u-nederlandse-vervoeging/#close (personal communication from Kari Koonin, 07.10.20).

In *The Story of Spanish* (2013: 361), Canadian researchers Nadeau and Barlow discuss the increasing number of *americanismos* (words used in the Americas) that now feature in the Spanish Academy's dictionary (15% of entries). The Castilian term for computer is *ordenador* (modelled on the French *ordinateur*), whereas the Latin American term is *computador*. There is even a Department of Urgent Spanish that works closely with the Real Academia and has suggested Spanish technological terms to replace English ones (such as la Red for the internet).

In the United States itself, the Prohibition era led to the **coinage** of various new words to describe new concepts that emerged between 1920 and 1933 as a response to the 18th amendment to the US constitution that banned the production, sale or transportation of alcoholic beverages. Many of these survive today. They include, for example, *speakeasy*, a place where alcoholic beverages were illegally sold (www.merriam-webster.com/words-at-play/prohibition-era-words/sp eakeasy) and the still commonly used *booze cruise*, which originally referred to a boat trip that sailed outside US jurisdiction (www.merriam-webster.com/words-a t-play/prohibition-era-words/booze-cruise).

PART 1: TEXT ANALYSIS

In this part we explore linguistic change, using the Quick Identification Guide to pinpoint new concepts and topics; new or innovative cultural, social or literary features; new, adapted or repurposed lexis; and grammatical change. These categories are fleshed out in Part 2 to provide a more detailed analytical framework, which can be used to analyse source and target texts or for the process of translation (in Chapter 3).

Quick Identification Guide

Topic/text type	subject and genre; new concepts, themes or ideas
Context/culture	new/innovative social, cultural or literary features
Language	new, adapted or repurposed lexis or grammatical change

Text 1: Culture

The text below is taken from *A New Era for Auctions? Christies is removing all barriers to introduce one mega-sale. What will the implications be?* (Mutual Art online, 19 May 2020).

Before reading the text, it is helpful to devise a strategy to tackle new or adapted lexis.

Strategy: there are **two main considerations** when navigating new or adapted language: i) *comprehension* – are the words clear in context? ii) *existing translations* – are there any translated versions of the unit? If so, are there several in your target language, just one, or are there none at all?

i) If the meaning of the unit is not clear in context, research in the source language is needed; if there is no definition of the unit readily available, finding existing source text examples that shed light on the intended meaning is useful; ii) Existing translated versions may be calques, literal translations, paraphrases, **glosses** or message-based **sense translations**. You may find some acceptable and others unacceptable. If you find none of the existing versions appropriate, you have three basic options: a) devise a translation yourself; b) leave the unit in the source language and provide a gloss; c) paraphrase or explain the unit in the target language. The choice of strategy at this point depends on the text type, space (possibly for a longer version), consistency and economy (paraphrase, gloss and explanation may lengthen the target text too much). A footnote may be appropriate, but only where the text **format** allows it, for example, in an academic piece of writing, provided that the article does not already contain footnotes. Translator's notes are an option but should be used sparingly. Where provided, a brief helps the translator to make decisions about providing explanatory additions.

In the following texts, some lexical units appear in bold indicating a new, adapted or 'house-style' form, such as a hyphenated compound or grammatical change. When you read the texts, consider the units in bold as translation challenges and imagine what strategy you might adopt in each case.

> In a **suspenseful announcement**, Christie's unveiled a new auction format over the weekend, promising drama and excitement for all participants. The auction will do away with **movement-dedicated night sales** as well as **the single-location event**, and pit Pablo Picasso against Roy Lichtenstein, Zao Wou-Ki against Ed Ruscha, by consecutively moving its **live events (in-person and online)** from Hong Kong through Paris and London, before climaxing in New York. The leading auction house aptly named the sale *ONE: A Global Sale of the 20th Century*, not only bringing attention to the merging of several sales, but also implying that this might be the first sale of a new globalized format that might define auction house practice in the **post-corona market**. So far, Christie's has only announced four lots for the July 10 sale — masterpieces by the above-mentioned artists, estimated collectively at $90 million. Three of the announced lots are assigned to the **New York finale**, whereas Zao Wou-Ki's *21.10.63* will lead the Hong Kong sale. Estimated at $10+ million, the painting "is the largest red painting from the artist's Hurricane Period, and is a dazzling example of the artist's power and virtuosity during the most energetic period of his career," according to the press release.

Comments

In terms of comprehension, **suspenseful announcement** is straightforward. The English word 'suspense' is a widely used loan word in Romance languages (though French also has *suspens*). *Suspense* (from the Latin *suspensus*) originally entered English via the Old French phrase *en suspens* (in abeyance), although its use in connection with the emotion generated by a thriller or drama is not attested before 1951. *Suspenseful* appears to be a handy (but awkward) extension to *suspense* (along the lines of *beautiful*) and instances of *suspensefulness* have even been found. In both cases some adaptation is needed, as in the following (rather curious) example from the French version of Linguee: a suspenseful plot/*un tracé de suspenseful* where the extended adjective has been 'nouned'.

In Italian, Linguee provides just two viable suggestions for suspenseful: *pieno di suspense* (paraphrase/sense translation) and *emozionante* (near synonym).

Complex compound forms in English are a standard lexical challenge in translation. Popular in technical and specialist texts, they also feature widely in advertising and usually need 'unpacking', not only for semantic reasons but also for transfer into the target language. Take **movement–dedicated night sales**, for instance: *movement* has nothing to do with auction logistics: it is a movement in art (or history) as the addition of *dedicated* suggests. Germanic languages are able to create similar compounds, but Romance languages and other ones would probably need to resort to paraphrasing in order to encompass all the different elements of the compound. **Single-location event** is easier to construe, given that the components are transparent. However, two paraphrases, in quick succession, are likely to affect flow and coherence. The adjectival form **in-person** (events) has gained in popularity as a neat way of distinguishing between physical and online attendance of an event, whether at an auction or in a virtual classroom. The phrase **post-corona** poses an interesting challenge: most media (and other online) sources in various European languages express this notion using the English phrase *post-COVID* (likewise *pre-COVID*). Thus, transferring the concept into another language may bizarrely result in one English form being replaced by another of the same meaning. The last phrase in bold – **New York finale** – is clear, though *finale* in English is itself a loan word (from Italian via Latin); in French, for example on Linguee, it generates the following paraphrase for translation of 'this event will be the finale of the project': *cet événement viendra couronner le projet*, where the translator may have felt that *la finale* was too narrow in meaning (i.e. the final event of a sports competition). Another entry on the same Linguee page suggests *point culminant* to translate the concept (www. linguee.com/english-french/search?source=auto&query=the+event+finale).

TASK 1

Translate Text 1 into your target language if you are a speaker of a language other than English. Make notes on the strategy you adopt for each of the units in bold and justify your choice of translation.

Group work: Discuss the notes you have made and the advantages or disadvantages of the solutions you have chosen.

If English is your L1, find a short text in your source language showing how the auction market or another cultural environment has changed due to the pandemic containing examples of new and adapted lexis. Translate the text into English and justify your translation solutions for the new/adapted lexis.

Group work: Compare the new/adapted vocabulary you have encountered in the texts you used. Make a glossary of any new words and phrases with translated versions.

Texts 2A and 2B: Politics and society

The next discussion focuses on the concept of 'woke' culture, which has political, social and cultural relevance. Two texts have been selected to show how the word is used – one from a reader's letter to *The Guardian* newspaper and the other reporting on a speech given by Barack Obama published on BBC online.

The word 'woke' (the past simple form of the verb *to wake* – at least historically) has been re-engineered and used to qualify nouns such as *culture* and *generation*. Wikipedia informs us that by the late 2010s, 'woke' had taken root and indicated "healthy paranoia, especially about issues of racial and political justice and has been adopted as a more generic slang term and has been the subject of memes" (quoting Charles Pulliam-Moore, 8 January 2016: "How 'woke' went from black activist watchword to teen internet slang", Splinter News, accessed 20 December 2019, https://splinternews.com/how-woke-went-from-black-activist-watchword-to-teen-int-1793853989).

Before reading the texts, check to see if 'woke' with this new connotation (often shown in English with speech marks) is used in languages other than English. Is it transposed in the English form or adapted in the target language?

Incidentally, the quirky form 'wokery' (usually found in inverted commas) has also emerged, as a label for the concept – especially when used by those critical of radical ideas.

Text 2A

Many people didn't **buy into across-the-board social liberalism**, or at least not fully, and now feel that the wind is blowing in their direction and are emboldened to vent their criticism.

But it's not enough just for liberals to recognise that this is what's happening and adjust their tactics accordingly. **The anti-woke people** have a point. It's not that they are right but that the emphasis we liberals place on having the correct attitudes towards feminism, homophobia, identity politics, and so on, is just not that important in their world. Many have far bigger fish to fry, like getting a job that pays a living wage, surviving on a pension or social security, finding somewhere to live, worrying about their health. Recognising a "woke" issue, deriving the correct behaviour to it, and adjusting one's own behaviour accordingly is, frankly, a luxury they can't afford and is irrelevant to their lives.

(Source: The Guardian online Identity Politics 3.2.2020 Letter from David Williams www.theguardian.com/society/2020/feb/03/being-woke-isnt-so-ea sy-even-if-you-know-what-it-means)

Comments

According to an article by Steven Poole in *The Guardian* online (25 December 2019), "the term 'woke', for example, is now used mockingly for a kind of over-righteous liberalism; but its first recorded use, by the African-American novelist William Melvin Kelley, was meant to indicate an awareness of political issues, especially those around race, a positive usage that still also persists" (www.thegua rdian.com/lifeandstyle/2019/dec/25/woke-to-gammon-buzzwords-by-people-coi ned-them).

The transition from a positive connotation to one used 'mockingly' but – at the same time – positively, shows only too clearly how words and phrases evolve over time, depending on who uses them, how and where. The **inference** that can be drawn from this process is that context is all-important for a correct interpretation of the 'semantic range' that writers attach to their use of buzzwords and their idiosyncratic usage of trendy words and phrases.

The expression *buy into across-the-board social liberalism* is certainly no buzz phrase, as a buzz phrase should be succinct and memorable to gain currency. This lengthy word chain incorporates various elements: a **phrasal verb**, a hyphenated lexical unit and a noun compound; these elements are sequenced into an extended lexical unit. As mentioned in the discussion on Text 1, cumbersome nominalised con- structions in English inevitably create specific translation challenges, often resulting in paraphrase and 'unpacked' sense translations in other languages. Social liberalism is a concept that has existed since the 19th century, while the use of *buy into* has split off from its original meaning of buying shares in a company to accepting, agreeing or identifying with something. Even though the more recent connotation of *buy into* has existed for some years, many machine translation (MT) versions produce literal versions of the phrase – usually inappropriate in context – suggest- ing that (at the time of writing) this connotation of the phrasal verb has not yet generated standard translated forms in other languages. The use of *across-the-board* (hyphenated here to describe social liberalism) dates back to around 1900 and was used to indicate a wager "in which equal amounts are bet on the same horse to win, place or show" (www.theidioms.com). As with *buy into*, the phrase has expanded: here, with the meaning of generalising and applying to all. Linguee 'hits' in different language combinations indicate that the more recent connotation is generally transferred using forms based on *general*. *The anti-woke people* obviously refers to anyone who does not subscribe to 'woke' ideas: if 'woke' is, at the time of writing, not aligned with standard 'equivalents' in translation, then 'anti-woke' may take longer to consolidate, thus generating a further translation challenge.

Text 2B

Former US President Barack Obama has challenged "**woke**" **culture** telling young people: "The world is messy." He made the comments at the Obama Foundation's annual summit in Chicago on Tuesday. Mr Obama said that **calling people out on social media** did not bring about change, and that change was complex. "Woke" is described as being alert to racial or social discrimination and injustice, along with being aware of what's going on in the community.

Mr Obama told the audience: "I get a sense among certain young people on social media that the way of making change is to be as judgemental as possible about other people. If I **tweet or hashtag** about how you didn't do something right or used the wrong verb, then I can sit back and feel pretty good about myself because **'Man did you see how woke I was**? I called you out!'"

(Source: BBC online: Barack Obama challenges "woke" culture 30.10.2020
https://www.bbc.co.uk/news/world-us-canada-50239261)

Comments

Text 2B also reports on reactions to the 'woke' culture, using a colloquial register to address a youthful audience familiar with social media. By referring to 'woke *culture*', Obama recognises that this ideology is now firmly entrenched and has become a social phenomenon in its own right. Importantly, he also recognises that change is complex and believes that comments on social media do not, in themselves, trigger change. What is interesting about the journalist's definition is that it is 'watered down' by a vague **generalisation** that contrasts with the more technical part of the description. As with other social media references, these are often transposed in European languages using the English term or an adapted form (e.g. *twittare* in Italian). In Italian, French and German *hashtag* is assigned the masculine gender. (For a list of French Twitter translations, see: www.frenchtoday.com/blog/french-vocabulary/french-vocabulary-for-twitter-vocabulaire-francais-pour-twitter). The phrase *call out* used to criticise someone or something is not exclusive to social media, and the connotation here probably developed from the notion of challenging someone to a fight. The final phrase in bold needs a highly colloquial rendering in the target language.

TASK 2

Find some examples of texts in languages other than English containing the following English terms: *trigger warning, entitlement, safe space, destatueing, privilege, denaming, hate speech, callout culture, virtue,* where used with reference to social media and/or the woke culture and social liberalism.

In the texts you have found, are these terms defined, glossed, paraphrased or translated? What assumptions does the writer make about the readership's ability to understand them?

Create a two-column glossary of English terms relating to cultural and social concepts used in social media and add comments in the right-hand column on versions of the terms in your source/target language.

Group work: Discuss your findings and pool your resources to produce an enlarged and improved glossary in your working languages.

Text 3: Environment

The text below is taken from an article entitled "Secrets of the ice: unlocking a melting time capsule" by Mike Power from *Guardian Weekly*, 6 November 2020 and originally published in *The Observer* on 1 November. The terms that appear in bold indicate that the expression is relatively new or, as in this case, is used in a new or emerging branch of science, namely glacial archaeology. When you read the text, consider the units printed in bold type as translation challenges and imagine what strategy you might follow in each case.

Context

In the introductory paragraphs, the journalist explains how, in 2018, archaeologists surveying a disappearing ice field in northwest Mongolia found a perfectly preserved 3,000-year-old arrow shaft in crumbling snow. They then uncovered the matching bronze arrowhead, presumably untouched since the Bronze Age. The report continues below:

> For generations, nomadic reindeer herders had used this *munkh mus* or "**eternal ice**" in summer months to cool their herds and offer them respite from the biting insects that plague these heights. And before written or oral history – before humans had domesticated animals – nomadic Mongolians had observed the reindeers' behaviour, and had lain in wait, ready to hunt.
>
> But in the summers of 2016 to 2018, ice patches in Mengebulag melted for the first time in living memory. Summer temperatures in Mongolia have increased 1.5C in the past 20 years – higher than the global average. And as the great thaw opened a window into a once inaccessible past, the archaeologists were overwhelmed by the sheer volume of material revealed: horsehair ropes, countless shafts, spears, the sinew of animals used for tying arrowheads and making bows, all intact, but all under imminent threat of destruction now that they were free of the ice.
>
> This is a story playing out worldwide as global heating gathers pace, creating a new academic discipline – "**glacial archaeology**". This, though, is something of a misnomer, says Professor Brit Solli, an archaeologist at Oslo University, Norway. "Most of the finds emerging from melting ice caused by climate change are not from moving glaciers, which tend to crush and destroy objects, but from large **ice patches**, which ebb and flow," she says. That said, some ice patches contain snow that fell over 10,000 years ago, meaning they also offer climate data in the same way as glacial **ice cores**.

Comments

Comprehension: the general meaning of the text is quite clear in the context although it combines two different fields of discourse: archaeology and glaciology.

Until we researched the terminology in greater depth, it was not evident that certain terms have a very specific meaning for glaciologists. Because this is an emerging science, you will find that dictionaries, even online dictionaries and corpora, are of limited use. What you need is lateral thinking and multilingual searching skills, such as identifying a keyword or name in the source text that can then be used as a starting point. The more specific you can be, the more effective your search will become. Academic publications are likely to be useful sources of information and sometimes it is worth looking at the list of references (i.e. the bibliography) at the end of a paper since this will often provide you with the term you were looking for.

Terminological research strategies

In order to demonstrate some of the online resources available and show you what they can and cannot offer, we have researched some of the technical terms in detail, explaining the strategies that you could adopt to research an emerging field in science or technology.

Term 1: eternal ice

The term was not found on IATE but a search on the Italian Linguee provided the terms *ghiaccio eterno, ghiaccio perenne* and *ghiacci eterni*. Most of these terms back-translated on the same site as 'eternal ice'. The German version of Linguee provided the term *ewiges Eis* and in French both the singular form *glace éternelle* and the plural form *glaces éternelles* were listed. For Spanish, Linguee provided *hielos eternos*, which in turn back-translated into the English source term.

Term 2: glacial archaeology

We first looked for existing translations. Although there were not any hits on IATE nor on the French or German versions of Linguee, an internet search on websites in French revealed that the term *archéologie glaciale* was used to describe this new science in the Autumn 2017 issue of the Swiss journal *l'Alpe* in an article by Philippe Curdy (*Ce que nous murmurent les glaciers: une nouvelle science émerge avec le réchauffement climatique: l'archéologie glaciale*).

Likewise, searches using the German term *Gletscherarchäologie* (not a direct equivalent since its **literal meaning** is *glacier archaeology*) produced a link to an article in German on a Swiss website for the bilingual Canton of Valais/Wallis (www.vs.ch/de/web/archeologie/archeologie-glaciaire).

No equivalents were found in the Spanish and Italian Linguee corpora but a search on the Spanish-language National Geographic site (https://ngenespanol.com) said with reference to Dr Lars Pilo that *Él dirige el Programa de Arqueología Glaciar en Oppland, Noruega*. This suggests that, like the German, the Spanish equivalent is a calque of *glacier archaeology*. A further search on Italian sites yielded an article by

Federica D'Auria on a University of Padua e-bulletin that mentioned *archeologia gla-ciale* (*Il ritiro dei ghiacci in Norvegia rivela un'antica via di comunicazione percorsa dai vichinghi*, 6 May 2020 https://ilbolive.unipd.it/it/news/ritiro-ghiacci-norvegia-rivela-unantica).

Term 3: ice patches

A term found on the French Linguee site was *bancs de glace* but back-translation into English using the same site indicated that this term could also mean *ice floes*, which suggests larger sheets of ice. IATE also cited *banc de glace* for the singular form *ice patch*. It gave *Eiskappe* as the German form. Back translation on IATE also gave 'ice cap' so this term seemed doubtful. In order to check how viable these suggestions were, we searched on English websites, leading us to the definition below:

The basic difference between a glacier and an ice patch is that a glacier moves, while an ice patch does not move much ... Ice masses can switch between being ice patches and glaciers over time. During a colder climate, like 'the Little Ice Age', ice patches could increase in size to a point where they became sufficiently thick (25–30 m) to start moving and turn into glaciers. Essentially all glaciers have started as ice patches (https://secretsoftheice.com/climate/glaciers).

By researching the names and then the publications of German-speaking experts in this field, we discovered that a Swiss Professor called Albert Hafner had written about *Gletscher und Eismulden* (www.pastglobalchanges.org/people/people-databa se/index.php?option=com_comprofiler&task=userprofile&user=5355&lang=en).
This turned out to be a red herring, however, since further reading of articles in both languages suggested that an *Eismulde* is a 'glacial trough'. At first glance it seemed that another possible equivalent of 'ice patch' could be *Eisfeld*, but further reading on the website created by Norwegian glacial archaeology specialists (https://secretsoftheice.com, accessed on 12.11.20), which also uses the term 'glacier archae-ology', indicated that there is a subtle distinction between a field of ice, an ice mass and an ice patch. So where should a translator working out of English into other languages go from here?

Much of the research appears to emanate from Norway and Switzerland, so we decided to focus on German in our analysis. A click on the drop-down menu 'Press' on this website and then a second click on the tab to the left of three pro-vided links to press articles published in various languages. We then browsed through one of the German articles about the ice-covered Lendbreen pass used by the Vikings entitled *Der eisige Pass der Wikinger*, which appeared on www.sp ektrum.de/news/der-eisige-pass-der-wikinger/1723096 on 16 April 20. Our search now yielded the term *Eisflecken* and back translation into English on the German Linguee then revealed 'patches of ice' for Eisflecken in the plural form and 'ice patch' for the singular form Eisfleck.

An IATE search for a Spanish equivalent provided us with *manchan de hielo*, which did back-translate as 'ice patch' but no equivalent could be found in Italian on either linguee.it or on IATE.

Term 4: ice cores

This translated into French on Linguee as *carottes de glaces*, a term that seemed to back-translate into the English source term and the same was true for the Italian *carote di ghiaccio*. In Spanish, the most popular hit on Linguee was *núcleo de hielo*, which in turn back-translated as 'ice core'. In German, Linguee listed both *Eisbohrkern* and *Eiskern*, both of which were listed as 'ice core' in a search on the German–English window.

No exact results were found on IATE but 'ice core research' was listed in French as *étude de carottage de glace*, and in German and Italian less accurate equivalents were given: *Kernbohrungen im Eis* and *prelievi di campioni di ghiaccio* respectively.

The same site listed *deep ice cores* in French as *carottage de glace profond*, which implies a process rather than the end result, in German as *Eisprobe aus tiefen Schichten* (= ice sample [*sic*] from deep layers) and in Italian as *nuclei profondi di ghiaccio* and Spanish as *profundos núcleos de hielo*.

TASK 3

If you are a speaker of a language other than English, first try to find a **model text** in your target language that matches the subject matter and register of Text 3 and then translate Text 3 into your TL. Make notes on the strategy you adopt for each of the units in bold and justify your chosen translation.

If your own target language is not covered by the languages featured in the examples, try in addition to find suitable sources of the terminology you might need if it does not appear in the model texts you have located.

Group work: Discuss the notes you have made and the advantages or disadvantages of the solutions you have chosen.

If English is your L1, find a short text in your source language about the melting of the glaciers and some of the remarkable discoveries that have emerged as a result. Highlight any examples of new or adapted lexis. Translate the text into English and justify your translation solutions for the new/adapted lexis.

Group work: Compare the new/adapted vocabulary you have encountered in the texts you used. Make a glossary of any new words and phrases and their target language (TL) equivalents.

Text 4: Working life

The next text looks at an area of the economy that has evolved rapidly in recent years – the so-called *gig economy*. The text is an extract from the article "From 'woke' to gammon: buzzwords by the people who coined them" by

Steven Poole (www.theguardian.com/lifeandstyle/2019/dec/25/woke-to-gamm on-buzzwords-by-people-coined-them)

Read Text 4 and identify potential translation challenges relating to the phrases in bold.

> For a long time, the "**gig economy**" sounded like a glamorous euphemism for a world of **zero-hours contracts** and piecework. Why worry that giant corporations such as Uber don't want to class their drivers as employees? If we're all doing "gigs", we're all **hip jazzers**. (The word "gig" – etymology unknown, remarks the Oxford English Dictionary – has meant a musical engagement since the 1920s.) But the phrase was originally coined as a criticism.
>
> On 12 January 2009, the journalist and editor Tina Brown wrote an article for the *Daily Beast* website, observing: "No one I know has a job anymore. They've got **Gigs**."
>
> Increasingly, people she knew who used to have staff jobs in the media were working in two or three part-time positions, or freelance. "To people I know in the bottom income brackets, **living paycheck to paycheck**, the Gig Economy has been old news for years," she added. "What's new, is the way it's hit **the demographic** that used to assume that a college degree from an elite school was the passport to job security." Now everyone was a member of "**the hustling class**", and company managers were "mesmerised by the notion that everyone can now be hired cheap – that everyone is **slave labour**". That was 10 years ago, and it looks awfully prophetic. When people began to use the word "gig" in this context, Brown says now, it worked to project **a subterfuge coolness over a predicament caused by an economic downshift**. It's cool to say, "I've got these gigs" rather than to say, "My main job has disappeared." Because of its cool sound, it helped to familiarise people with the phenomenon.

Comments

As with the previous texts, the strategy needed to tackle translation challenges focuses mainly on meaning and **localisation**. Definitions are always useful, and sometimes critical, although these may differ according to context (e.g. country, culture, subject area). Information on how new or adapted terms are used in practice in the source language and culture/s is also key to grasping the meaning of a lexical unit and applying it to the linguistic and cultural target context. Identifying new, unclear or ambiguous terms before starting to translate, especially where these are key terms, helps to form a coherent strategy.

According to the website *wired.co.uk*, the key term *gig economy*

> gets its name from each piece of work being akin to an individual "gig" although such work can fall under multiple names. It has previously been called the "sharing economy" — mostly in reference to platforms such as

Airbnb — and the "collaborative economy". However, at its core are app-based platforms that dole out work in bits and pieces — making deliveries, driving passengers or cleaning homes — leading some to prefer the term "platform economy".

(www.wired.co.uk/article/what-is-the-gig-economy-meaning-definition-why-is-it-called-gig-economy)

Other languages refer to the gig economy using the English term (or a slightly adapted version as in the German *die Gig-Economy* or the Spanish *Economía Gig*); alternatively, a paraphrase or sense translation is used. Spanish versions found include *trabajo esporádico, trabajo temporal* and *economía de rebusque*. Italian and French tend to use the English form: *la gig economy*.

The American expression *living paycheck to paycheck* (now also common in British English) implies spending all the money you earn before your next paycheck (or salary) is due, thus making it virtually impossible to save money; consequently, anyone losing their job is likely to experience cash flow problems. Translated versions in European languages tend to be calques or adaptations of the phrase. Another economic expression: *zero hours contract* (a contract between an employer and a worker in which the employer is not required to ensure a minimum quota of hours) is another phrase that lends itself to calque or simple paraphrasing in translation.

However, the American phrase *hip jazzers* is a different kettle of fish: although it may appear curious, it is simply a compound of *jazzer* (jazz musician) and *hip* (cool). That said, the allusion is not entirely clear in context. Thus, is it sensible to attempt to explain the intended meaning using a gloss? There are risks involved in this strategy, and if the text does not justify **expansion** it may be better to avoid speculation.

The term *demographic* appears to be a relatively new noun, according to the Merriam-Webster dictionary: "Today *demographic* is also being used as a noun; so, for example, TV advertisers are constantly worrying about how to appeal to 'the 18-to-24-year-old demographic'" (www.merriam-webster.com/dictionary/dem ographic). Here, the function is clearly nominal, but in combination with another noun (e.g. *demographic change*) its grammatical function may be less clear.

Phrases within inverted commas usually sound alarm bells and '*the hustling class*' is no exception. *Hustling* has various uses in connection with work; it may indicate making money illegally or unfairly, or aggressive business practices. Confusingly, *hustle* is also a form of modern dance, so one could attend a *hustle* or *hustling class*; this connotation is, of course, a 'red herring' and would not fit the context.

The use of *slave labour* in this context may appear dramatic, even excessive. From a sociohistorical reference, this phrase has evolved to signal poor working conditions, typically ones with hard work and low pay. This connotation may appear to be frivolous and disrespectful to workers who suffered appalling conditions in colonial environments, for example, but working conditions in western European countries in certain locations and industries may, indeed, be described as slave labour with good reason. The complex description used by Tina Brown "a subterfuge coolness over a predicament caused by an economic downshift" shows only too well how words can hide a stark reality.

TASK 4

Group or individual work: In your opinion, which of the lexical units in bold in Text 4 would be the most challenging to translate, and why?

Without a translation brief, what assumptions would you make about the **target readership**, and how would these assumptions inform your translation strategy?

Texts 5A and 5B: Fiction

In Chapter 1 we mentioned that we would look at some contemporary fiction, and where better to start than with Young Adult writing? We consider two short texts, both of which are taken from a 2020 promotional booklet of Young Adult fiction extracts published by Usborne. Text 5A is an extract from S.M. Wilson's sci-fi book *The Library at the End of the Universe* (published by Usborne in April 2020). Text 5B is an extract from Holly Bourne's *The Places I've Cried in Public* (October 2019, from the Usborne promotional booklet).

5A Context

Ash, a young female pilot, wants to enter the Star Corporation Academy and is taking part in a competition with other candidates to win a place there. As you read through the passage, try to visualise the action as if watching a film or gaming sequence.

> Her gaze flicked left, then right, scanning the darkness for another tiny distortion. There it was. Up to the far right of her vision.
> She yanked the stick towards her, throwing the nose of her fighter upwards as she let out a stream of fire. This time the enemy craft had barely started to materialize from its jump before it disintegrated into a million splinters. For a split second, she saw a flash of red against the pale hull – the sign of one of the fighters from Corinez. Her mouth instantly dried as shards of metal shot around her, a few spearing the hull of her fighter.
> There was a ping. Two orange lights. She glanced at the screen in front of her. Potential hull breach. And fuel leakage. The biggest crises for a fighter pilot. Loss of fuel could leave her floating in space for the rest of her natural life.

5A Comments

The novelty value of the author's style lies not so much in her use of new or adapted vocabulary, but in the way she renders speed and action by 'dynamic' words such as *flicked, yanked, materialize, jump, disintegrated, splinters, flash, instantly, shot, spearing, ping, glanced, crises, floating*. Most of these words are verb forms, which in sequence build a dynamic forward thrust. Another device to suggest immediacy is found in the last paragraph, in the use of short staccato sentences, following Ash's impressions as they rush through her mind.

5B Context

Amelie has moved home and is starting a new school. She has left her boyfriend Alfie behind and is feeling sad. As you read the text, identify elements of style and language that differ from standard use.

> I piled into the front seat of our hot car and it was like climbing into an uncomfortable hug. My legs smudged sweat onto the leather. Summer was reluctantly hanging on, apparently missing the memo that it was now September. We pulled out of the communal car park and I turned the radio up.
> Mum turned it down again. "Are you sure you're going to be okay walking home? Call me if you get lost."
> "Mum, there are these things called phones. They have maps on them now and everything."
> "Well, you can still call."
> We drove along streets I didn't know, rounded corners I didn't know, drove past students I didn't know, who were on their way to the same college as me that I didn't know. They walked in clumps, while I shrank into my seat. We got stuck in traffic as cars struggled to find parking spaces.
> Exhaust smoke fugged its way through the car's air conditioning, making it smell of pollution.
> "I may have to spit you out here," Mum said.

5B Comments

This text, like 5A, narrates a sequence of events. But here the action is delivered through Amelie's eyes and impressions, not by a third person narrator. The first three sentences each contain an unusual use of language in context (*uncomfortable hug; smudged sweat; missing the memo*), which add a novel upbeat sound to the discourse. The dialogue is prosaic, yet Amelie's sarcasm betrays a sense of unease and annoyance. The serial repetition of 'I didn't know' emphasises the sense of alienation she feels, while the final description of pollution seems a metaphor for Amelie's black mood.

TASK 5

Group or individual work: Which of the two texts 5A and 5B do you think would be more challenging to translate? Are the challenges mainly lexical or stylistic? What kind of background research would be useful to help devise a translation strategy?

Text 6: Technology

The text below is taken from an article by Steve Ranger, published in 2019 on www.zdnet.com/article/what-is-hyperloop-everything-you-need-to-know-about-the-future-of-transport/, which describes Egon Musk's Hyperloop concept.

What is Hyperloop? Everything you need to know about the race for super-fast travel

The basic idea of Hyperloop as envisioned by Musk is that the passenger **pods** or **capsules** travel through a tube, either above or below ground. To reduce friction, most – but not all – of the air is removed from the tubes by pumps. Overcoming air resistance is one of the biggest uses of energy in high-speed travel. Airliners climb to high altitudes to travel through less dense air; in order to create a similar effect at ground level, Hyperloop encloses the capsules in a reduced-pressure tube, effectively allowing the trains to travel at airplane speeds while still on the ground. In Musk's model, the pressure of the air inside the Hyperloop tube is about one-sixth the pressure of the atmosphere on Mars (a notable comparison as Mars is another of Musk's interests). This means an operating pressure of 100 pascals, which reduces the drag force of the air by 1,000 times relative to sea level conditions and would be equivalent to flying above 150,000 feet.

How do Hyperloop capsules work?

The Hyperloop capsules in Musk's model float above the tube's surface on a set of 28 **air-bearing skis**, similar to the way that the **puck** floats just above the table on an air hockey game. One major difference is that it is the pod, not the track, that generates the air cushion in order to keep the tube as simple and cheap as possible. Other versions of Hyperloop use magnetic levitation rather than air skis to keep the passenger pods above the tracks.

The pod would get its initial velocity from an **external linear electric motor**, which would accelerate it to "high subsonic velocity" and then give it a boost every 70 miles or so; in between, the pod would coast along in near vacuum. Each capsule could carry 28 passengers (other versions aim to carry up to 40) plus some luggage; another version of the pods could carry cargo and vehicles. Pods would depart every two minutes (or every 30 seconds at peak usage).

Comments

Comprehension

For a translator without a background in transport technology to understand the text, it would be useful, if not vital, to have access to diagrams or photographs. Technical translators frequently need to have recourse to visual aids of this kind in order to understand this process but anyone who has ever worked with patents will be aware that the drawing is often hard to follow. With new technologies that are still in development, this could also be the case. When we researched this technical field, we were luckily able to find various clearly labelled diagrams, photographs of prototypes and a short video clip online. The technology was also featured on Wikipedia sites in various languages, which could be a useful starting point for terminological research.

Terminology

In technical translation, one of the key problems is that the same terms can have widely different meanings depending on the specific technical field in which they are used. One of the most often cited German examples is *Dichtung*, which in everyday parlance means 'poetry' or 'literature' but can be either a 'gasket', a 'seal' or a 'packing' in various fields of engineering.

Likewise, the English word '**pod**' is polysemic (i.e. it has many possible meanings). The Cambridge dictionary lists the following: "the long, narrow, flat part of some plants, such as beans and peas, that contains the seeds and usually has a thick skin"; "a long, narrow container that is attached to an aircraft for carrying engines, weapons, extra fuel, etc"; "a small simple building, or a small simple structure in a building, often rounded in shape"; "group of sea mammals such as whales or dolphins" (http s://dictionary.cambridge.org/dictionary/english/pod accessed on 14.01.21). In this case, the second definition comes the closest to the sense implied here.

In the present text, a **capsule** suggests a passenger-carrying container that is considerably larger than is suggested by the traditional definitions given in the Oxford dictionary, namely: "a small case or container, especially a round or cylindrical one", and "a tough sheath or membrane that encloses an organ or other structure in the body, such as a kidney or a synovial joint".

The term **air-bearing skis** presents further challenges to the translator, who may wonder if the term 'bearing' is a noun or a gerund, because this could impact on how to render it in the target language. Further research confirmed that it is a noun since air bearings are the kind of bearings that use compressed air. We found an article on www.omniamfg.com/mechanical/2020/10/20/how-things-work-the-hyp erloop which explained that the skis "generate an air cushion for near friction-less gliding along the track".

Puck is a sporting term from ice hockey used to describe the small, hard rubber disc that is used instead of a ball. A quick check for the equivalents cited on Linguee suggests that German uses *Puck*, French uses *palet*, and Italian and Spanish both use *disco*.

A **linear electric motor** is like the propulsion system used on maglev (magnetic levitation) trains. The main challenge for a translator with limited knowledge of transport technology is understanding the concept but there are fortunately a number of websites dedicated to explaining how things work. For instance, a post by Chris Woodford on www.explainthatstuff.com/linearmotor.html defines linear motors as "electric induction motors that produce motion in a straight line rather than rotational motion". Equivalents found on Linguee were French: *moteur linéaire*; German: *Linearmotor*; Italian: *motore lineare* and Spanish: *motor lineal*.

TASK 6

On 8 November 2020 Virgin Hyperloop successfully tested a full-scale model of its Hyperloop system with two human passengers.

See if you can find model texts in your source and target languages which will provide you with the terminology that you could use to create a small bilingual or multilingual glossary for Hyperloop technology.

Search tip: Look for the Press tab on the site https://virginhyperloop.com/ and you should find press releases and articles in English. To find parallel articles in your own target language, change the settings in your search engine to limit your search to texts written in the language you need.

PART 2: ANALYSIS OF TRANSLATED TEXTS

Translators need to be aware of how language adapts and changes, in both source and target language texts, and in which particular fields. How quickly do resources used by translators keep abreast of changes and where can such information be found? Which new words or phrases are particularly crucial, or challenging for translators, in general or in specific cases? Where there is no corresponding word or phrase in the target language, what options are available to the translator?

Our Guidance Table is designed to be universally applicable, rather than confined to English, French, German, Italian and Spanish, and we hope that if you translate or interpret between English and Arabic, Chinese or Russian or indeed any other language, you will find the Table equally useful to help you evaluate and document new developments in your target language and culture.

Any new terms identified when applying the Table to a source text can be added to your personal glossary of new terms and target language equivalents, which will become an invaluable working tool for both new and experienced practitioners.

This Table is based in part on our analytical models introduced in *Thinking English Translation* and in *Translation: A Guide to the Practice of Crafting Target Texts*. The practical Table we propose prompts you to respond more fully to the source text by identifying key areas and points that are crucial for comprehension and translation. It can be used in a time-constrained professional or academic context (for example, an urgent professional translation, a translation exam or assignment) or to generate a more detailed and in-depth scrutiny of the source text prior to translation. (See Chapter 3 for examples of translations with commentaries.)

The three translated extracts selected for this part are indicative of social and/or linguistic change. The Quick Identification Guide in Part 1 provides an initial simple and effective way of highlighting new concepts and language in texts and identifying translation challenges, particularly in terms of research and strategy. The Guidance Table drills deeper into the source text by prompting a response to questions about the text, while providing a framework for comparing source and target texts.

Guidance Table

Criteria	Description	Prompts
Subject/theme	Content/domain/ideas/concepts	What is the text about? Are there new ideas/concepts? Are you familiar with the domain/content? Research needed?
Purpose/use/brief	Information/instructions	What is the translation for? Is any information or brief provided clear?
Genre/format	Type of text; physical form/layout	Are you familiar with the genre/specific format required? Are there any images/diagrams? Do you have the technical skills?
Target readership	Specific or presumed recipients of the translation	Who is it for? If not stated: what assumptions can be made?
Context/culture	Social/cultural/literary/scientific context of ST	Are there any new/innovative social, cultural or literary features? Any **extra-contextual** references or concepts? Are timeframes standard or unusual?
Language	Grammar/syntax/lexis/register/punctuation	Is there any new, adapted or repurposed lexis or grammatical change? Is there any use of **idiolect/sociolect**/dialect/neologisms/calques/loan-words/invented or third language words and/or phrases?
Meaning	Sense of discourse; meaning of single units/whole text	Is the meaning clear? Is there any ambiguity?
Viewpoint	Subjectivity/objectivity of message/opinions/bias	Single or multiple viewpoints? Any persuasive/political angle?

Texts 1a and 1b

Texts 1a and 1b are extracts taken from French former government minister Azouz Begag's 1986 memoir *Le Gône du Chaâba*, and from *Shanty-Town Kid*, a translation of this work by Naïma Wolf and Alec G. Hargreaves into American English (2007). The book tells the story of Begag's childhood in Lyon during the 1960s and demonstrates both cultural and linguistic changes. A major challenge in producing the target text would have been the large number of borrowings from the Arabic used by Algerian immigrants.

The passage chosen describes his first meeting with Monsieur Loubon, his class teacher when he goes up to the lycée and is the only Arab student in the class. Both have experience of French and Algerian cultures but from opposite ends of the spectrum. In the course of their conversation, the teacher refers to Algerian Independence, which was gained in 1962, after a long struggle.

Text 1a	Text 1b
- Moi aussi, j'habitais en Algérie. A Tlemcen. C'est près d'Oran. Vous connaissez?	I too used to live in Algeria. In Tlemcen. It's near Oran. Do you know it?
- Non, m'sieur. Je ne suis jamais allé en Algérie.	No M'sieur. I've never been to Algeria.
- Eh bien, vous voyez: moi je suis français et je suis né en Algérie, et vous, vous êtes né à Lyon mais vous êtes algérien.	So, let's see. I am French, but I was born in Algeria, and you are born in Lyon, but you're Algerian.
Il sourit avant de poursuivre:	He smiled before continuing:
- Je suis venu en France quelque temps après l'indépendance.	"I came to France some time after Independence."
- Alors, vous êtes un pied-noir, m'sieur? lui dis-je en connaisseur.	"So, you're a pied-noir, M'sieur? I said to him, showing my knowledge.
- Un rapatrié d'Algérie, oui. On dit pied-noir aussi.	"A repatriated citizen from Algeria, yes. One can also say pied-noir."
Puis de la tête, il m'invita à poursuivre mon idée.	Then, nodding his head, he invited me to carry on with what I was saying.
- Quand mon père habitait à Sétif, il travaillait chez un patron qui était pied-noir aussi. C'est lui qui me l'a dit. Même qu'il s'appelait Barral.	"When my father worked in Sétif, he worked for a boss who was also a *pied-noir*. He told me that. I even know his name: Barral."
- Qu'est-ce qu'il faisait votre père, à Sétif?	"What did your father do in Sétif?"
- Il était journaliste dans la ferme de Barral ...	"He was a journalist on Barral's farm."
- Journaliste? Dans une ferme? interroge le prof, ébahi.	"A journalist? On a farm? The teacher asked, amazed."
- Oui, m'sieur. Il gardait les moutons, il s'occupait des chevaux, il travaillait la terre, toute la journée.	"Yes, Sir. He looked after the sheep, and the horses, he worked on the land, all day long."
- Il éclata de rire avant de dire:	He burst out laughing, then said:
- Ah! Vous voulez dire qu'il était journalier?	"Oh! You mean he was hired as a journeyman?!"

- Je ne sais pas, m'sieur. Mon père dit toujours qu'il a été journaliste. Alors moi je répète ce qu'il me dit.	"I don't know, Sir. My father always said he was a journalist. I'm just repeating what he said."
- Non, non, reprend-il, on dit journalier. Mais vous savez, tous les pieds-noirs n'avaient pas de ferme comme Barral en Algérie ...	"No, no," said teacher (sic). "The correct word is *journeyman*. You know, not all *pieds-noirs* owned a farm like Barral in Algeria."
- Je ne réponds rien. Tout ce que je sais, c'est que mon père dit que les « binoirs » n'aiment pas les arabes, et surtout ce qui travaillent avec lui, à l'usine.	I said nothing in response. All I knew was that my father said that the *binoirs* (*pieds-noirs*) didn't like the Arabs, especially those who worked with him in the factory.

Comments

Language

The term *pieds-noirs* has been transferred into the target text because there is no direct English equivalent for this sensitive term, which was widely used to denote people of French and European origin born in Algeria during French colonial rule. As Alec Hargreaves points out in the preface to the translation, Monsieur Loubon is not a typical *pied-noir* (white settler). He clearly misses the country of his birth and is keen to point out that not all *pieds-noirs* owned farms. At the same time, he prefers to describe himself as "*Un rapatrié d'Algérie*", possibly because he considers *pied-noir* to be potentially pejorative.

Context and culture

Begag celebrates cultural diversity by "using multiple linguistic registers", peppering his prose with words in Algerian Arabic (Hargreaves 2007: xvii). The register the boy adopts when speaking to his teacher differs considerably from the language used to describe how his friends and family spoke. In an attempt to replicate the pronunciation of Algerian immigrants, he tells us that his father refers to *binoirs*. (In an appendix to his memoir, the author explains that there is no letter p or v in Arabic.) The author and the translators have attached a gloss in order to bridge the gap created by this non-standard pronunciation.

Meaning

Another interesting feature of this extract is the confusion over the job Azouz's father had when he lived in Algeria. The translators opted for the rather **archaic** term "journeyman", which is not a direct semantic equivalent because a "journeyman" is defined in the *Collins English Dictionary & Thesaurus* (2000 edition) as a "craftsman, artisan, etc., who is qualified to work at his trade in the employment of another" or as "a competent workman". The Collins French–English dictionary (www.col linsdictionary.com/dictionary/french–english/journalier) gives the meaning of *journalier* as "a day labourer". The prime consideration when deciding how to craft the target text effectively would have been to preserve the unintentional play on words, rather than to find the rendering closest in sense to *journalier*, which would have resulted in a far greater translation loss.

Texts 2a and 2b

Texts 2a and 2b are edited from public information in both languages provided on the website of the Italian Council of Ministers relating to COVID-19 prevention measures (Source: http://www.governo.it/it/articolo/comunicato-stampa-del-consiglio-dei-ministri-n-90/16024).

The words that appear in bold are commented on below the texts.

Text 2a	Text 2b
Il Consiglio dei Ministri ha approvato un nuovo decreto-legge che introduce ulteriori disposizioni urgenti per il contenimento della diffusione del COVID-19. Il testo proroga lo stato di emergenza al 30 aprile 2021.	The Council of Ministers approved a new decree-law on further urgent provisions for the containment and prevention of the Covid-19, extending the state of emergency to 30 April 2021.
È consentito, una sola volta al giorno, spostarsi verso un'altra **abitazione privata abitata**, tra le 5.00 e le ore 22.00, a un massimo di due persone ulteriori a quelle già conviventi **nell'abitazione di destinazione**.	A maximum of two people may travel to another **inhabited private home** between 5 a.m. and 10 p.m., once a day, in addition to those already living in the **dwelling of destination.**
La persona o le due persone che si spostano potranno comunque **portare con sé i figli** minori di 14 anni (o altri minori di 14 anni sui quali le stesse persone esercitino la potestà genitoriale) e le persone disabili o non autosufficienti che con loro convivono.	The person or the two persons travelling may, however, **take with them their children** under 14 years of age (or other children under 14 years of age over whom they exercise parental authority) and any disabled or dependent persons who live with them.
Tale spostamento può avvenire all'interno della stessa Regione, in area gialla, e all'interno dello stesso Comune, in area arancione e in area rossa, fatto salvo quanto previsto per gli spostamenti dai Comuni fino a 5.000 abitanti.	**Travelling** may take place within the same Region, in the yellow area, and within the same Municipality, in the orange area and in the red area, except for the provisions for travel from Municipalities with up to 5,000 inhabitants.

Comments

The challenges of translating texts for the general public into English are well-known: i) the variety of target-language cultural settings (unless specified by the client or translation provider); ii) the more complex and impersonal style and register employed by many source texts, for example in the Romance languages – in particular Italian and Romanian, which both tend to adopt a (conventional) position of greater distance from the target audience, which is often at odds with conventions for the same type and function of text aimed at English-speaking targets);

iii) any **restructuring** considered essential by the translator may end up creating more problems than it solves! It is worth remembering that in emergencies the need to get out information to the target audience quickly and clearly is paramount, as mentioned in Chapter 1.

In Box 1, three TT solutions merit a comment: i) in British English it would be more 'natural' to use the present perfect (*has approved*) rather than the simple past, particularly at the beginning of the text, though American English does not make much use of the present perfect tense for past references. ii) The decree-law is not *on* urgent provisions; it *introduces* them: *on* used in this sense incorrectly implies the subject matter of the measure. iii) The translation of *diffusione* as *prevention* is curious and suggests that the translator may have been offered an edited source text compared to the one here. It is not uncommon to find source texts edited or updated for translation, therefore no longer in step with an earlier published text that appears 'in parallel' with the translation on a website.

In Box 2, *a.m.* and *p.m.* replace the 24-hour clock (generally used across Europe while the 12-hour clock is used in the USA, Canada, Australia, New Zealand and a few other countries). Where translators are not provided with specific information about the target culture, they will probably use the conventions with which they are most familiar. The restructuring of the sentence here is not entirely successful since the direct link between the persons travelling and their children is lost and only added in later. That said, the ST is tortuous and hinders the need to set out information clearly. An *inhabited private home* sounds odd, but at least the meaning is clear and while the *dwelling of destination* is also clear, it sounds very awkward indeed! One might assume that if time can be taken to restructure the sentence, a better way could be found to express this latter concept!

Box 3 shows further evidence of awkwardness in expressing the concepts: *take with them their children* is a **literal translation** and could be replaced with *may be accompanied by their children*.

Box 4 suffers from too many commas, which fragment the word flow, partially obscure the message and require greater effort from the reader to navigate the information. Starting the sentence with *Travelling* is not helpful and the link to the *fatto salvo* phrase is not effective because of comma interference. However, the translator was 'in a cleft stick', as to stray from the impersonal form and move to a direct form of address – often used in English when giving instructions or advice – would be too 'radical' for the context.

Text 3

Text 3 is a contemporary German fable in rhymed verse for children titled *Keine Stille Nacht*, written and illustrated by Bettine Koch, which intrigued poet John Gohorry so much that he decided to translate it into English in collaboration with the author. The translator decided on a novel approach to the translation: by 'amplifying' the German text he produced an English version that he describes as a 'rendering'. He comments:

The narrative direction and overall structure of the poem are kept, and I've tried to capture the form, rhythm and rhyme – even the tone – of the original. At the same time I have not held back where I felt that small embellishments would be in keeping with, and would underpin, the overall character of the original in an English context.

(Keine Stille Nacht/Not a Silent Night, *Bettine Koch*
[translation: John Gohorry], 2017)

The excerpt is the first verse of the book.

Text 3a	Text 3b
Seit Tagen schon hat es geschneit Und bald, ganz bald ist Weihnachtszeit. Sehnsuchtsvoll schaut in den Garten Max und kann es kaum erwarten Einen Schneeman dort zu bauen Statt zum Fenster rauszuschauen! Aber viele Schüler haben, Wie auch er, noch Hausaufgaben! Wütend stampft er mit dem Fuss, Weil er Vokabeln lernen muss.	Snow's fallen, deep and thick and white for days and days, and Christmas night is what Max thinks of, sadly staring across the gar- dens he'd like sharing with snowmen, snowballs, skates and slides, igloos, ice- palaces, ice-rides. But like most children Max must stay indoors and not go out to play; his teachers have all set him work, hard exercise he must not shirk.

Comments

This English adaptation of the German text is included not so much because it features new or repurposed lexis, but due to the innovative way in which the translator, John Gohorry, formats and processes the message and storyline. He uses a technique throughout the translation known as **domestication** (which brings the target text into line with the target culture). This adapted poetic 'vehicle' enables him to approach cultural challenges without the usual constraints. The names of some characters are kept, while others are changed; Christmas delicacies popular in Germany (*Mandelsterne, Pfeffernüsse, Butterstollen* and *Spekulatius*) are transformed and replaced with foods that evoke the spirit of a traditional 'English' Christmas, such as cinnamon, spice, candied peel, mince pies and Yuletide logs. This innovative 'freedom' of approach to the English version reflects the concept of **transcreation**, defined by us in *Thinking English Translation* (Cragie & Pattison 2018: 37):

> The process of transposing source content into target content involves a creative effort on the part of the translator that is beyond purely linguistic intervention. The aim is to deliver a product that is fit for purpose in expressing the information, ideas and emotions of the message, thereby meeting the expectations of the target context.

In Chapter 3 we focus on the translation process, selecting source texts that show evidence of new, adapted or repurposed language. The translations are accompanied by commentaries from the translators, explaining how they approached the translation task and arrived at the target text solutions.

3

TRANSLATING AND COMMENTARY WRITING

In this chapter we show how lexical challenges relating to new and changing sociocultural phenomena are reflected in translations in four language pairs (English/French, German/English, Italian/English and Spanish/English). To explain how they approached specific challenges in their translations, the translators provide a list of comments and/or a written commentary, based in part on the Guidance Table and in part on the research and translation skills discussed in the two previous chapters. The Table provides a lead-in to the translation process by prompting reflections on strategy and problem-solving.

All four source texts provide details of the context and a translator's brief. An overview of how to write a commentary for a translation appears in Chapter 4.

Each set of translations and comments is complemented by practical tasks designed to elicit responses to specific lexical, cultural and professional aspects of the source and target texts.

Text 1: English into French

Context: The following text is a summarised version of the blog *Travel Trends in 2021: what to expect from the future of travel after Covid-19* by Jennifer Phillips, published on the Smartvel website. The blog updates travel agents on predicted changes in the travel industry. (Source: https://blog.smartvel.com/blog/travel-trends-in-2021-what-to-expect-from-the-future-of-travel-after-covid-19; accessed February 2021.)

Brief: Translate for an international forum assessing the consequences of the pandemic on the travel industry.

DOI: 10.4324/9781003136903-4

Due to the pandemic, travel organizations have found themselves highlighting cleaning protocols, eliminating change fees, and keeping travelers informed of changing regulations. Airlines like United, Iberia, and JetBlue experiment with different cleaning protocols that include touchless technology at baggage check-in and electrostatic pistols that shoot a disinfecting powder in the cabin to clean everything, including headrests and armrests. Airlines have also eliminated change fees to encourage travelers and implemented new tech solutions to keep them aware of border regulations.

En raison de la pandémie, le secteur des voyages a été amené à mettre en avant les protocoles de nettoyage, l'élimination des frais de modification et l'information des voyageurs sur les nouvelles réglementations. United, Iberia, et JetBlue font partie des compagnies aériennes qui testent différents protocoles de nettoyage, notamment la technologie sans contact à l'enregistrement des bagages et les pistolets électrostatiques qui pulvérisent un désinfectant dans la cabine pour tout nettoyer, y compris appuis-tête et accoudoirs. Les compagnies aériennes ont également supprimé les frais de modification des billets pour encourager les voyageurs et mis en œuvre de nouvelles solutions technologiques pour les tenir au courant des règlements frontaliers.

Reassurance is a continuous theme in 2021 tourism: highlighting cleaning protocols, social distancing, and staying up to date with entry restrictions and border regulations will continue to be necessary. Digital Health Passports and Contactless technologies will help.

Rassurer le public est un thème constant du secteur touristique en 2021: accent mis sur les protocoles de nettoyage, distanciation physique et actualisation de l'information sur les restrictions à l'entrée et les règlements frontaliers continueront d'être nécessaires. Les passeports numériques de santé et les technologies sans contact seront utiles.

The blend of business travel and leisure continues being a travel trend. More people want to travel slower and get to know local communities where they do travel. Business travelers want to have a human back up in case of complex travel issues. However, for the initial booking, they're likely to do it themselves. According to Business Travel Trends, 63% of travelers prefer to book their own travel. Likely, this reflects a general shift as millennials now represent roughly 50% of the workforce.

Combiner déplacements professionnels et loisirs reste une tendance du secteur des voyages. Les gens sont plus nombreux à vouloir voyager plus lentement et apprendre à connaître les communautés autochtones partout où ils vont. Les voyageurs d'affaires souhaitent être épaulés en cas de complications liées à leur déplacement professionnel. En revanche, ils s'occupent généralement eux-mêmes de la réservation initiale. En effet, selon les tendances en matière de voyages d'affaires, 63 % d'entre eux préfèrent réserver leurs propres déplacements. Cette évolution traduit sans doute un changement général, les milléniaux représentant désormais environ 50 % de la population active.

Contactless technologies are here to stay. Now that everyone has hand washing and germs on their minds, keyless entries and digital menus have found a place in the travel eco-system. The pandemic has only accelerated the adoption of these across the travel industry.

Les technologies sans contact sont vouées à perdurer. Maintenant que chacun se préoccupe du lavage des mains et des microbes, les entrées sans clé et les menus numériques ont trouvé leur place dans l'écosystème des voyages. La pandémie n'a fait qu'accélérer leur adoption dans tout le secteur.

As we look into the crystal ball for travel predictions, we know that people are likely to be cautious. If experience is any indication, the travel industry will return. Those who stay engaged with customers now and reassure their safety will reap the rewards when those customers choose to travel again. The future of travel will include reassurance in many ways. Just as 9/11 changed travel, the pandemic will leave travelers more aware of health measures.

En cherchant à prédire les futures tendances en matière de voyages, nous savons une chose: les gens seront enclins à la prudence. Si l'on se fie à l'expérience passée, le secteur des voyages rebondira. Ceux qui maintiennent le contact avec leurs clients aujourd'hui et garantissent leur sécurité récolteront les fruits de leurs efforts lorsque ces clients décideront de voyager de nouveau. L'avenir des voyages passera à bien des égards par l'offre de garanties. Tout comme le 11 septembre a transformé les voyages, la pandémie rendra les voyageurs plus conscients des mesures sanitaires.

Commentary

This is an extract from a blog by Jennifer Phillips informing the reader of predicted changes in the travel industry following the COVID-19 pandemic. Its main function is informative and as such the text contains industry-specific terms such as *change fees* and some technical terms reflecting the growing importance of technology in future travel, such as *touchless technology*. The style is informal with some non-standard phrasing (*to travel slower*) or unusual collocations (*reassure their safety*). For clarity and naturalness, the few metaphors in the ST (*shoot a disinfecting powder, look into the crystal ball*) may be best treated on the basis of their sense rather than translated literally. The words *travelers* and *travel* are frequently used, sometimes within the same sentence, which will require different strategies in the TT in order to avoid clumsy repetitions. The spelling of *traveler* denotes US English usage.

The term *change fees* is an example of an industry-specific term that does not seem to have found its way into dictionaries and official terminology databases yet. For example, the only record found on Termium ("modification du barème des cotisations") is from the field of productivity and profitability and is irrelevant here. This illustrates the instability of newer vocabulary and required more refined searches on airline websites. While Air France referred to *change fees* as "frais de dossier", Royal Air Maroc used "frais de changement" and other airlines simply mentioned that a ticket was "modifiable sans frais". In the end the translator chose the more transparent "frais de changement" over "frais de dossier" which, out of its Air France context, might come across as unclear.

Are *touchless technology* and *contactless technology* the same thing? In France at least, the answer so far is yes. In English, *touchless technology* refers to devices and systems designed so that people avoid physically touching surfaces that may have been contaminated, while *contactless technology* is mostly used in the context of card payments. In French the phrase "sans-contact" seems to cover both (see: *L'évolution des technologies sans-contact après le confinement* [chefdentreprise.com]). It may be that because the concept of *touchless technology* is relatively new no new term has been coined for it in French, so a word with a similar meaning has been used instead. It could just be that French does not have two words to convey the differences in usage like English has and so uses the nearest available one ("sans-contact"). For this reason, the translator has used "technologies sans contact" for both *touchless technology* and *contactless technology*.

In French translation (and in other languages too), there are a number of micro strategies to avoid clumsy repetitions. In this case, the frequency of use of *travel/travelers* within the same sentences called for such strategies. In some instances, synonyms have been used (*get to know the local communities where they do travel* > "apprendre à connaître les communautés autochtones partout où ils vont"; *business travel* > "déplacements professionnels"). Another technique consists of doing away with the repeated word altogether where this does not affect clarity: *keyless entries and digital menus have found a place in the travel ecosystem. The pandemic has only accelerated the adoption of these across the travel industry.* > "[...] les entrées sans clé et les menus numériques ont trouvé leur place dans l'écosystème des voyages. La pandémie n'a fait qu'accélérer leur adoption dans tout le secteur".

The word *reassurance* refers both to words spoken to appease or reassure and the guarantees or assurances given to back up those words (e.g. stricter cleaning procedures). In this text the noun *reassurance* and the verb *to reassure* have alternatively been conveyed as "rassurer" and as "garanties (offertes)" depending on the specific meaning of each of their occurrences. Also, regarding the sentence *Reassurance is a continuous theme in 2021 tourism*, the translator felt that only by expanding the sentence and adding an object to *reassurance* did the French make sense. Hence "Rassurer le public est un thème constant du secteur touristique en 2021". As for the unusual *and reassure their safety*, the verb "garantir" was chosen instead of "rassurer" in order to achieve a valid collocation in French: "et garantissent leur sécurité".

The passage *electrostatic pistols that shoot a disinfecting powder* is an example of new technology-related terms. While a direct equivalent in French was easy enough to find online for this type of new cleaning tool, the phrasing of the rest of the sentence was slightly more challenging. It seemed to make more sense for the translator to render *disinfecting powder* with a more generic "désinfectant" and to compensate the loss of *powder* by translating the ST verb *shoot* as "pulvériser", which not only conveys accurately the idea of spraying a substance onto surfaces, but is also derived from the Latin for powder (pulver;-eris).

Sources of terminology and/or model texts: https://aircanada.com; www.airfrance.fr › achat › frais_dossier_airfrance www.france24.com› *202103... (2021)* Covid-19: la Chine lance "un passeport santé" numérique (france24. com); www.frenchbee.com; www.larousse.fr/dictionnaires/francais/pulv%C3%A9riser/65074; www.larousse.fr/dictionnaires/francais/mill%C3%A9nial/188370; www.royalairmaroc.com; www.voyages-d-affaires.com; https://www.voyages-d-affaires.com.

TASKS

1. If you translate from English into a language other than French, after reading the translator's commentary decide whether the ST challenges identified by the translator also require a problem-solving strategy in your TL. If so, suggest an appropriate strategy.

2. If you translate into English, identify five ST words or phrases that the translator has commented on and search for corresponding terms in your SL. Where French is your only SL, make an extended French/English glossary of the words and terms in the ST/TT and supplement it with other lexis relevant to post-pandemic travel and tourism.

Text 2: German into English

Context: The following text is a report by Andreas Schweiger outlining the content of a paper presented at the international online conference on *Sprache im Lockdown* (Language in Lockdown), which was held at the University of Graz, Austria, in December 2020 (https://sprache-im-lockdown. uni-graz.at/de).

In the presentation, which was published on the University of Graz website in December 2020, linguistics researcher Elisabeth Scherr described a research project analysing the linguistic features of German media reports of the pandemic.

Brief: Translate for an international forum on cross-cultural communications and language change.

Was das Virus mit der Sprache macht: Germanistin[1] der Universität Graz zeigt Einfluss auf mediale Berichterstattung auf

Das Corona-Virus beeinflusst unser Handeln. Es verändert sogar unsere Kommunikation. Elisabeth Scherr[2] Germanistin an der Universität Graz, hat herausgefunden, dass sich die vor allem zu Beginn der Pandemie starke Ungewissheit massiv in Medienberichten widerspiegelt. Bei ihrer Studie standen Modalverben wie *sollen, können* und *dürfen* im Fokus, die Unsicherheiten buchstäblich zur Sprache bringen können.

What the virus is doing with language: a German language specialist[1] at the University of Graz demonstrates its influence on media reporting

The coronavirus is affecting our behaviour. It is even changing how we communicate. Dr[2] Elisabeth Scherr, a German language specialist at the University of Graz, discovered that the huge uncertainty that was particularly prevalent at the start of the pandemic was very widely reflected in media reports. Her study focused on modal verbs such as *sollen* (ought to / be thought to), *können* (to be able to) and *dürfen* (to be allowed to/may), which can literally be used to express uncertainties.

Etwa 500 Artikel der Online-Ausgaben der Tageszeitung „Der Standard"[3] mit dem Schwerpunktthema Corona[4] hat Elisabeth Scherr für ihre Studie untersucht: „Es hat sich gezeigt, dass mit Februar 2020 zunehmend häufig grammatische Strukturen, die eine Vermutung ausdrücken, eingesetzt wurden." Die Wissenschafterin am Institut für Germanistik führt dies auf die unklare Faktenlage insbesondere zu Beginn der Pandemie zurück.

Diese Situation kommt unter anderem durch die Verwendung von Modalverben zum Ausdruck. „Dort *soll*[5] eine mittlerweile als, Patientin 31' bekannte Person dutzende Menschen angesteckt haben", nennt Scherr ein Beispiel aus der Zeitung „Der Standard" vom 24. Februar 2020. Ebenso häufig tauchen in den Artikeln die Modalverben „dürfen" und „können" in dieser Weise auf.

Je länger die Pandemie dauert, desto besser die Datenbasis. Das schlägt sich in der Berichterstattung nieder. „Denn im Vergleich zum Februar 2020 ist die Verwendung der so eingesetzten Verben im Oktober 2020 signifikant gesunken", bestätigt die Forscherin. In Ergänzung zu den „Standard"-Artikeln analysierte Scherr diese „Vermutungsstrukturen"[6] in der deutschen „Bild"-Zeitung[3]. Der Vergleich dieser beiden Medien ergab einen deutlichen Unterschied in Bezug auf die Nennung von Quellen, wenn Modalverben zum Ausdruck einer Vermutung in Berichten über das Corona-Virus verwendet werden.

Scherr: „In der Bild-Zeitung wurden sie in den analysierten Berichten immer wieder ohne Quellenangabe verwendet, im Standard in den überwiegenden Fällen mit."
Wie facettenreich Ungewissheit auf Sprache wirken kann, zeigt Elisabeth Scherr anhand des vielzitierten Satzes von Sebastian Kurz vom 30. März 2020: „Bald wird jeder von uns jemanden kennen, der an Corona gestorben ist."

Die Wissenschafterin[7] erläutert die Effekte, die sich durch die grammatische Gestaltung ergeben: "Die Wirkung dieses Zitats wird maßgeblich dadurch beeinflusst, dass das Verb im Futur verwendet wird, was das sichere Eintreten eines Szenarios nahelegt."

For her study, Dr Scherr, an academic at the Institute for German Language Studies, examined around 500 articles from the online editions of the Austrian quality daily newspaper "Der Standard"[3] in which coronavirus[4] was the main topic. "It transpired that, as of February 2020, grammatical structures that express uncertainty were used increasingly," she said. She attributes this to uncertainty over the facts, particularly at the start of the pandemic.

This situation is expressed among other things by using modal verbs. She quotes an example from the newspaper "Der Standard" of 24 February 2020, which said that a person known as 'patient 31' is thought to (*soll*)[5] have infected dozens of people. The modal verbs "dürfen" (may) and "können" (can) likewise appear in the articles just as often.

The longer the pandemic lasts, the better the database will be. This is reflected in the media reports. Elisabeth Scherr confirmed, "This is because, compared with February 2020, the use of verbs employed in this way declined significantly in October 2020." In addition to the articles from the "Standard", she analysed the use of these "Vermutungsstrukturen"[6] (grammatical devices that indicate speculation) in the popular German newspaper "Bild"[3]. A comparison of these two media showed a clear distinction regarding the naming of sources when modal verbs are used to express an assumption in reports about coronavirus.

Dr Scherr added: "In the *Bild*, sources were repeatedly used without a citation in the reports we analysed, but in the *Standard*, in the majority of cases, sources appeared with a citation."
Dr Scherr demonstrates how diverse the effects of uncertainty on language can be by referring to the much-quoted statement by Sebastian Kurz made on 30 March 2020: "Soon each of us will know someone who died of coronavirus."

She[7] explains the effects that result from the grammatical forms used: "The effect of the quote is largely influenced by the fact that the verb is used in the future tense, which suggests that the occurrence of a given scenario is a certainty."

Die Ergebnisse ihrer Studie stellte die Germanistin kürzlich bei der internationalen Online-Tagung "Sprache im Lockdown", veranstaltet als Kooperation der Institute für Germanistik sowie für Sprachwissenschaft an der Universität Graz, vor.	Dr Scherr recently presented the results of her study at the international online conference "Language in Lockdown", jointly organised by the Institute for German language studies and the Institute of Linguistics at the University of Graz.

Comments

[1] **Equivalence:** A lexical equivalent for *Germanistin* does exist in English in the form of a *Germanist* but this term is rarely used outside the highest echelons of academia. Nowadays we would refer to a *German language specialist*.

[2] **Cultural background:** There are some cultural differences between the ways German and English sources refer to academics. In the source text there are no details of the researcher's status, but an online search revealed that she has a doctorate. It would be considered courteous to include her title in the English target text.

[3] **Context:** The English-speaking reader needs to be informed of the nature of the two publications used as the basis of this research project so information that is implicit in the German text needs to be made explicit in the English version by referring to *der Standard* as an Austrian quality daily newspaper.

[4] **Neologism:** German speakers refer to *Corona* but in English we would refer either to *coronavirus* or to *COVID-19*.

[5] **Exegesis:** Because the crux of this linguistic research project was to investigate the use of modal verbs, in particular *sollen, soll* needed to appear in the text with a brief explanation or exegesis. The first chosen rendering was *is said to,* but this was changed to *is thought to* in order to avoid repeating *said.*

[6] **Theme:** As in the case above, the German term *Vermutungsstrukturen* was retained in the target text because it encapsulates the main theme of the research. There is no direct semantic equivalent that incorporates both of the constituent parts of this compound noun. In English the most appropriate term would be *assumptions* or *speculation*. Some English grammars (such as www.youtube.com/hashtag/bbclearningenglish) refer to 'modals of speculation' to describe verbs used in similar contexts. The strategy adopted here was to transfer the German term so that readers could look up this research online, adding a gloss in brackets to explain the English meaning.

[7] **Meaning:** To avoid repetition, the author of the source text has used a technique known as elegant variation, referring to *die Wissenschafterin* ('the academic') rather than using a pronoun, as the translator has done. In the next paragraph, she is referred to as *die Germanistin* ('the German language specialist'), which we replaced with her name. A literal translation that introduces a new noun or two new nouns might well confuse an English-speaking reader, who would expect the name of the researcher to be repeated or to be substituted by a pronoun. For stylistic reasons, we chose to use a pronoun. This example highlights the difference in perceptions of what constitutes good style in the two languages – whereas in English we use pronouns, in German (and in many other languages), it is common practice to find other ways of repeating the same idea, that is, using a synonym or synonymous phrase. For the sake of **clarity**,

the information linking Dr Scherr to the German studies department was moved up to the beginning of the paragraph, a technique known as **fronting**, and it was placed in apposition with her name, replacing a definite article (the) with an indefinite article (an) in order to comply with English grammatical requirements.

TASKS

1. In your opinion, how useful are the details provided in the Context and Brief for directing and developing the translator's approach to the translation process in this case?

2. *Individual or group work:* Where no context or brief is provided for a translation, what kind of problems might arise for the translator?

3. Re Comment 1: Can you think of (or find) any context in which the term *Germanist* could be used? Comment on any related register issues.

4. Re Comment 7: In this comment, the term *elegant variation* is used. Is this strategy standard in your target language for dealing with repetition? If so, give some examples; if not, in your language combination how does a translator deal with repetition where reproducing it would be problematic?

Text 3: Italian into English

Context: The following text is an edited extract from the article *Il retail dopo il Covid 19: sei tendenze per i consumi della fase 2* by Cristina Lazzati, published in the *Affari e Finanza* section of *La Repubblica* online on 20 April 2020. The article reports on work done by Bain & Company on predicting future trends in retail (www.repubblica.it/economia/rapporti/osserva-italia/trend/2020/04/20/news/il_retail_dopo_il_covid_19_sei_tendenze_per_i_consumi_della_fase_2-254514182).

Brief: Translate for a virtual international conference on the post-COVID 19 retail sector.

Quale sarà l'impatto della pandemia sui consumi?	What impact will the pandemic have on consumer spending?
Il **lockdown**[1] ha incentivato la spesa online. La distribuzione (grande e piccola) si è attrezzata in tutti i modi possibili, facendo sì che la consegna a domicilio entrasse **a tutto campo**[3] nelle case degli italiani ma se il fermo terminerà, il ricorso all'e-commerce invece rimarrà. "E l'aumento dell'online va però di pari passo **all'ultra-prossimità**[3], ossia tempi di consegna più rapidi, disponibilità del prodotto e offerte personalizzate" spiega Andrea Petronio [*della Bain & Company*].	The lockdown[1] has galvanised online sales. Distribution centres large and small have deployed all the resources at their disposal, making home deliveries to Italian households **the centrepiece**[2] of their strategy. But while the lockdown will eventually come to an end, e-commerce is here to stay. "However, the increase in online sales needs to be combined with the '**ultra-proximity**'[3] retail concept, which means focusing on faster delivery times, product availability and customised solutions," explains Andrea Petronio [*at Bain & Company*].

L'attenzione alla sostenibilità di filiera, già presente nel periodo pre-Covid, prende anche le nuance del neo-patriottismo[4], quindi, attenzione alla provenienza e al Km0[5], vissuto oltre che come garanzia di freschezza e salubrità, anche in termini di solidarietà con la comunità di appartenenza.

Continuerà la solidarietà, incontrastata protagonista di marzo 2020, più attenzione ad anziani e persone in difficoltà e maggiore riguardo verso le attività di beneficienza e volontariato. I consumatori saranno particolarmente attenti al 'non essenziale', incrementando il ricorso alla *sharing economy*, a beneficio anche di un pianeta che "respira meglio/meno inquinato".

La vita in famiglia ha fatto riscoprire alcune abitudini andate perdute, **il ritorno in cucina non sarà momentaneo**[6] Abbiamo scoperto anche una nuova modalità di socializzare da Facetime a Skype, il trionfo di Zoom e così gli houseparty continueranno. E poi lo smart working, per molti una prima volta, è entrato d'imperio nelle vite aziendali, stabilendo nuovi rapporti, un diverso modo di dialogare e una maggiore familiarità con gli strumenti informatici.

Rimarrà come **"conditio sine qua non"**[7] la richiesta di **sicurezza**[8], la salubrità prende le vesti dell'igiene, della pulizia richieste al prodotto (e ai punti di vendita). Sicurezza anche informatica: l'apertura allo smart working rende le reti più aperte, quindi più fragili; così come il ricorso al home-banking, alla carta di credito, le rassicurazioni in merito alla sicurezza saranno fondamentali per garantire un rapporto duraturo postcovid. Secondo Bain & Company, nella neo-normalità vedremo dunque un "desiderio crescente degli shopper per un'esperienza in-store più 'amplificata' che unisca anche sicurezza e 'magnificenza' dello stare assieme."

Supply chain sustainability, already present in the pre-COVID era, is also **linked to localism**[4], as provenance and **zero-kilometre food production**[5] are important and experienced not only as a guarantee of freshness and hygiene, but also as solidarity with a community's roots.

Solidarity – the undisputed protagonist of March 2020 – will persist. There will also be a greater focus on older people and those experiencing difficulties, on charities and volunteer organisations. Consumers will be increasingly aware of what is 'non-essential' and turn to the sharing economy, which also helps the planet to "breathe more easily and be less polluted".

Family life has revived some long-lost habits and **home cooking will continue to be popular**[6]. We have also discovered a new way of socialising whether on Facetime or Skype; Zoom will reign supreme and virtual house parties will thrive. Smart working (a new experience for many) has revolutionised corporate life, promoting new relationships, a different way of communicating and greater familiarity with IT.

Safety and security[8] will remain **an absolute priority**[7] while thorough cleaning and hygiene are needed to protect both products and points of sale. Digital security is also crucial: smart working has opened up networks and made them more vulnerable. Security is also vital for online banking and credit cards to ensure a lasting post-Covid working relationship. According to Bain & Company, the new normal means that "shoppers will want an 'enhanced' in-store experience, combining safety and security with the great pleasure of being together".

Comments

The text makes predictions about post-COVID consumer spending and behaviour. The concepts are not new in themselves, but the way some references are used is novel or unclear and requires cultural, political or technical research. The words in square brackets have been inserted for clearer **contextualisation**.

[1]**Synonymy:** In the first line the English term **lockdown** is used in the ST then replaced by *il fermo*. Italian, like other Romance languages, often uses synonymy for 'elegant variation'. The other English terms in the text: *e-commerce* and *sharing economy*, show a typical Italian propensity for using English terms (particularly technical or specialist ones). Rather than finding a synonym in the TT for *il fermo*, **lockdown** is repeated here, as it is sufficiently remote from the first reference and unambiguous.

[2]**Metaphor – a tutto campo:** the sentence containing this common SL metaphor is rather unwieldy, so one option is to recast it to avoid awkward encoding. The chosen solution *Distribution centres (large and small) have deployed all the resources at their disposal, making home deliveries to Italian households the centrepiece of their strategy* reduces the ST length by a third. The extended form of the subject (*distribution centres*) works better in English, particularly with the possessive adjective, while the metaphor *a tutto campo* is replaced by a typical business phrase (*centrepiece of their strategy*).

[3]**Neologism – ultra-prossimità:** technically speaking, the (similar) English term *ultrasonic proximity* refers to sensors capable of detecting the presence of nearby objects or movements without physical contact using ultrasound, but the context here is different. Research suggests that the Italian phrase is adapted from a French term used by the Auchan logistics giant, indicating a diverse range of on-site customer services provided by their supermarkets, such as cafés, print shops for photos from mobiles or tablets, ordering bespoke foods and meals, home deliveries, TV and news broadcasts. The idea of 'proximity' here is that customers find the things they need *locally*, in one place.

[4]**Meaning – neo-patriottismo:** the term *neo-patriotism* apparently emerged in the US following 9/11 and is defined, in no uncertain terms, as "a blind flag-waving, galvanized, xenophobic and self-righteous public ready to follow a belligerent government into war against abstract concepts and arbitrary market competitors" (according to www.everything2.com/title/neo-patriotism). More generally, it implies right-wing populism. In the ST the term is used loosely and blandly to suggest a sense of local pride and autonomy, as exemplified by the list following the term. *Localism* captures the meaning in context and is preferred to the more extreme and ambiguous political term.

[5]**Abbreviation – Km0:** *KM0* or *0KM* (zero-kilometre) is a concept that originated in Italy and stands for food produced, sold and eaten locally, where the food products have (metaphorically) travelled zero km. The benefits are ecological; quality; freshness; non-polluting; no time lag between production and market; no added profit margins. If the readership is assumed to be retail-specific, the abbreviation Km0 or 0Km could be used.

[6]**Recasting – il ritorno in cucina non sarà momentaneo:** the ST phrase would benefit from recasting as the literal translation of *momentaneo* would sound odd in context. In particular, the fragmentary structure of the ST sentence creates the need for greater coherence.

[7]**Third language – "conditio sine qua non":** the Latin phrase (commonplace in Italian) needs replacing with a sense translation that expresses the concept emphatically yet naturally at the same time.

[8]**Ambiguity – sicurezza:** Italian does not distinguish lexically between the concepts of 'security' and 'safety', using *sicurezza* in both cases. The fragmentary nature of the ST and lack of clear structure and **cohesion** causes problems of coherence. The references to cleaning and hygiene are relevant to public health, therefore to safety rather than security. The other references – to IT, banking and so on – are more relevant to *security*. The decision was made to use both *security* and *safety*, where appropriate, rather than just *security*.

TASKS

1. If you translate from English, is the term *lockdown* current in your TL? Are there synonyms in your TL for it? If so, how many can you find? If *lockdown* is not used in your TL, how would you translate it?

2. If you translate into English, how many synonyms or similar terms in English can you find for *lockdown* to avoid repetition?

3. *Individual or group work:* In general, how do you deal with neologisms in your translation work?

4. *Individual or group work:* Discuss the changes to the retail sector caused by the coronavirus and say how your TL has adapted to these changes.

Text 4: Spanish into English

Context: The following text is an extract from the article *Covid, finde, faláfel, vigoréxico … Las nuevas palabras del Diccionario de la Lengua en 2020* by Luis Alemany, which appeared in the culture section of the online edition of *El Mundo* on 30 November 2020

(www.elmundo.es/cultura/literatura/2020/11/24/5fbcf1eefc6c83351e8b4577.html).

Brief: You have been asked to translate this extract for a publisher intending to update a Spanish/English dictionary.

La Real Academia Española (RAE) ha presentado la cosecha anual del Diccionario de la Lengua Española (DLE)[1], una actualización de su versión digital que ha incorporado 2.557 novedades, entre adiciones de artículos y acepciones y enmiendas[2].	The Real Academia Española (RAE) recently published the new entries for 2020 in its online Diccionario de la Lengua Española (DLE)[1]. Amongst the innovations – 2,557 in all – are new words and new meanings for existing entries, as well as revisions[2].

En las últimas ediciones del Diccionario fue muy relevante la incorporación del nuevo vocabulario político. Este año, aunque el énfasis se ha puesto en el lenguaje sanitario, hay también novedades en este campo: Entre las entradas nuevas o renovadas aparecen las palabras: **izquierdizar, libertarismo, movilizador, partitocracia, prebendarismo, enfeudamiento, parafascista o fascistoide[3]**.

Significantly, recent editions of the DLE have incorporated new political terminology and 2020 is no exception, although considerable emphasis has naturally been placed on language to do with medicine and healthcare. With regard to politics, the DLE now includes the following neologisms or words which have been repurposed.

Enfeudamiento
  [(n.m.) [3] – subjugation/enfeoffment][4.1]

Fascistoide
  [(adj., derogatory use) – tending towards fascism][4.2]

Izquierdizar
  [(v. trans) – to move to the left][4.3]

Libertarismo
  [(n.m.) – right libertarianism][4.4]

Movilizador-a
  [(adj.) mobilising]

Parafascista [4.5]
  [(adj.) *parafascist*]

Partitocracia
  [(n.f.) partitocracy/particracy]

Prebendarismo
  [(n.m.) prebendalism/ favouritism /patronage]

La palabra **derechoso**, documentada sólo desde 1997, se reencuentra por fin con su némesis, **izquierdoso**, incluida en el Diccionario desde la edición de 2001. La definición de izquierdoso ha sido corregida para que sea paralela a la de derechoso.

The adjective *derechoso* [right-leaning], only documented in the DLE since 1997, finally confronts its nemesis *izquierdoso* [left-leaning, derogatory use][4.6], which first appeared in the 2001 edition of the DLE. The definition of *izquierdoso* has been revised to appear as the antonym of *derechoso*.

En el Diccionario aparecen también palabras de contenido sanitario que no están directamente relacionadas con el coronavirus. Por ejemplo, el adjetivo **vigoréxico**, que se añade al sustantivo vigorexia[5], reconocido desde la edición de 2000. Su significado no es ningún misterio, pero su historia es curiosa. Vigorexia viene del inglés, bigorexia, que, a su vez, se escribe con b porque viene de *big*. [6] ¿Por qué en español se escribe con V? Por la cercanía con el sustantivo vigor.

New words related to medicine and healthcare not directly linked to the coronavirus pandemic are also listed in the updated DLE. One example is the adjective *vigoréxico*, appearing alongside the noun *vigorexia*[5], the latter first acknowledged in the 2000 edition. Its meaning is not obscure, but its history is strange. *Vigorexia* is a corruption of the English "bigorexia", which starts with a 'b' because its first etymon is 'big'[6]. However, the Spanish word has a different morphology: it starts with a 'v' as it is assumed to be derived from the noun '*vigor*'.[6]

Comments

Macro strategy

The genre of the SLT is 'newspaper article' and its purpose is to inform the readers of *El Mundo*, a Spanish broadsheet newspaper, which is relatively conservative in its outlook, about the 2020 edition of the *Diccionario de la Lengua Española*. This edition includes many newly coined words and phrases, or words and phrases that had fallen into disuse but are now making a comeback, and which are given the official stamp of approval by the *Real Academia Española*, the publisher of the dictionary. The journalist's stance is objective in this short passage and there is no observation or speculation about how or when the words came into use in Spain.

In contrast to the ST, the TT is destined for a much narrower readership: a publisher intending to produce an updated version of a Spanish/English dictionary. The purpose of the TT is informative (as is the purpose of the ST), but the translator has to consider the knowledge and needs of the TL reader specified in the brief, which are very different to those of a broadsheet newspaper reader.

Creating a TT that is a lively and 'interesting read' would be a primary consideration if the TL target readership had been a broadsheet newspaper reader and a freer approach would be adopted to improve style and flow. However, given the intended use of the ST material, a more pragmatic approach was adopted. The main aim is to compile an accurate update of a Spanish/English dictionary and to make it a commercial success. Therefore, a few additions were made so the final TT satisfies its intended lexicographical purpose.

With regard to presentation, were this a 'real-life commission' the completed translation would be sent to the client with additions in square brackets, to distinguish these from the translation itself (in black), including a translator's note to explain this strategy.

For an additional fee, on the basis that some research goes beyond the translator's remit, a file could be provided with links to relevant websites, and quotes from newspapers, journals or other authoritative sources giving examples of usage of the Spanish words could be included in the updated DLE. (See 4 below.)

Micro strategies

[1] **TT reader knowledge**: As target readers are likely to be familiar with Spanish culture, the title of the dictionary was transferred directly as *Real Academia Española* and *Diccionario de la Lengua Española* accompanied by the respective acronyms. Had the target readership been broadsheet newspaper readers, therefore arguably less knowledgeable, a translation and/or a gloss for both these terms would be provided.

[2] **Lexis**: *Artículo* has a wide semantic range and can be translated literally as 'article'. Given the context, however, it is a false friend; *artículo* means 'entry [in a dictionary]'. Coincidentally, an online dictionary has an ideal example of this usage:

No hay un artículo para esa palabra en el diccionario de la RAE ('There's no entry for that word in the RAE dictionary'): spanishdict.com/translate/articulo.

Enmiendas could be translated as its close equivalent 'amendments' or even 'emendations' but, taking into account the language used by the OED when describing updates, 'revisions' seems more appropriate in context (public.oed.com/updates).

[3] **The brief**: The order in which the words are listed in the TT has been altered because of its purpose. The target reader's task of updating a dictionary will be much easier if words are set out in alphabetical order. Recognising that the target reader is interested in the finer points of grammar (for example, gender of nouns and transitive/intransitive verbs) and is aware of the importance of context and **connotation**, parts of speech were specified after checking each word in the online edition of the DLE. This decision was reinforced by checking articles in English about updates to the OED, for example bbc.co.uk/news/newsbea t-50052420. In this BBC article entitled "Simples, whatevs and Jedi added to Oxford English Dictionary", parts of speech are given in each instance, as are details of usage in some cases.

[4] **Translation and elucidation**: Given the assumptions about the target readership, a suggested translation for each word is provided in the TT and, as mentioned in **Macro strategy** above, a file could be provided with examples of usage or a brief discussion from an authoritative Spanish source, preferably online, so it can easily be checked. The translation and file could be sent to a lexicographer or etymologist for reference to decide which English word is the closest counterpart to the Spanish. As a first step, online information about the OED was checked (public.oed.com/updates) for recent entries. There appeared to be no new entries regarding political terminology equivalent to the new entries in the DLE mentioned in the ST. The latest update of the OED is for March 2021 – in fact after the publication of the ST article – when new words and phrases included 'essential worker', 'gender pay gap' and 'me too'. A range of websites was also used to check for translations of the words in Spanish, and for additional clarification regarding usage. The online editions of the DLE and OED were, of course, very useful.

[4.1]*enfeudamiento*: https://mymemory.translated.net/en/Spanish/English/enfeu damiento. This website offered four short passages in Spanish on one side of the page with translations on the other; in the examples given, four different nouns were used as translations for *enfeudamiento*: 'feudatory', 'subjugation', 'enfeoffment' and 'power'.

[4.2]*fascistoide*: Servimedia.es/noticias/1335401. This website was a helpful resource which discussed some of the new additions to the DLE and contained the following quote: *'fascistoide' se define como un adjetivo despectivo para señalar a quien 'tiende al fascismo o al autoritarismo'* (i.e. 'fascistoide' is described as a pejorative adjective meaning someone who 'has a tendency towards fascism or authoritarianism'). The OED's definition of 'fascitoid' is quite closely aligned with this: 'tending towards fascist beliefs, attitudes, and practices; reminiscent or characteristic of fascism'. From the quotes in the OED, it is evident that 'fascitoid' has been in use in the English language for some time; significantly one of the quotes was dated 1936.

[4.3]*izquierdizar*: www.expansion.com/opinion/2020/11/26/5fbed8b9468a eb33738b4647.html. This source provides an in-depth analysis of the political significance of this word under the headline: *"La RAE acepta la palabra clave en España: izquierdizar"* (The RAE accepts the key word in Spain: *izquierdizar*).

[4.4]*libertarismo*: The online DLE defines *libertarismo* as *anarquismo* but 'anarchism' is not considered an appropriate definition in English: although the two concepts of 'anarchism' and 'libertarianism' are allied they are not synonyms; see: www.lib ertarianism.org/columns/anarchism-libertarianism-two-sides-same-coin.

It seemed that, given Donald Trump's period in office which ended on 20 January 2021, the Spanish word *libertarismo* included in the 2020 DLE was associated with his right-wing political philosophy. The OED proved helpful for checking the accuracy of this connotation and providing an appropriate translation for *libertarismo*. The first entry under 'libertarianism' defines it as 'the doctrine or belief that human beings possess free will' but a subsequent entry explained how, within politics, the term has taken on a different connotation:

> *Politics* (originally *U.S.*). A political philosophy advocating protection or expansion of individual rights, especially those connected with the operation of a free market, and minimization of the role of the state. This philosophy is generally associated with the political right.

Therefore, to translate 'libertarismo' as 'libertarianism' was too simplistic and the term 'right' was needed as a prefix. Wikipedia – not the best source – but undeniably useful, and constantly under revision, provided further elucidation: *"Right-libertarianism*, also known as *libertarian capitalism* or *right-wing libertarianism*, is a political philosophy and type of libertarianism that supports capitalist property rights and defends market distribution of natural resources and private property".

[4.5]*parafascista*: 'parafascist' is not included in the OED but it appears in Wiktionary; the hyphenated forms 'para-fascist' and 'para-Fascist' are also listed.

The term parafascism appears in online academic articles about Spain, for example Óscar Rodríguez Barreira's "The Many Heads of the Hydra: Local Parafascism in Spain and Europe, 1936–50" in the *Journal of Contemporary History* https://journals.sagepub.com/doi/abs/10.1177/0022009414538476.

[4.6]*Izquierdoso*: Servimedia.es/noticias/1335401. According to the ST, the meaning of *izquierdoso* has been changed, so it is *paralela* "parallel" to *derechoso* but it is more precise to describe the two words as antonyms (in other words, opposites).

[5] **TT reader knowledge**: The ST was reformulated and simplified to '*vigorexia* is a corruption of ... "bigorexia"'. As the TL reader is assumed to be well-informed, no explanation for the term is needed. Had the target been a broadsheet newspaper reader, the OED's definition for 'bigorexia' would have been provided: 'muscle dysmorphia'. The OED lists the **etymons** of bigorexia as the adjective 'big' and the noun 'anorexia' and cites one of the examples of usage (dated 2006): 'Media images of perfectly formed male bodies have been linked ... with reverse anorexia or "bigorexia", the excessive concern about being big or muscular'.

[6] **Style**: The rhetorical question in the SLT '*¿por qué se escribe …?*' has not been used in the TT. But for broadsheet newspaper readers, a similar form could be used: 'Why does the Spanish word start with a 'v'?' or made into a statement, drawing the reader in: 'You may well ask why the Spanish word starts with a 'v'.' Given the prime consideration (see notes under **Macro strategy**), the stylistic flourish was abandoned and a simpler structure was also chosen to introduce the linguistic terminology ('morphology' and 'etymon').

TASKS

1. The translator discusses the relevance of the Brief to their decision-making process on transferring the dictionary entries. Produce a summary of the criteria for a) a broadsheet newspaper readership, and b) the editor of the updated Spanish/English dictionary.

2. *Group work:* Discuss whether you think the translator's decision to attach a file to the translation containing extra material for the client should be considered 'part of the job' or whether it should be paid for separately? At what stage should this be decided?

3. In a recently published dictionary in your TL, search for neologisms and new entries and say whether you think the definitions are helpful or may need subsequent updating in a few years' time.

4

TRANSFERABLE SKILLS

In the first three chapters, we looked at language change and considered how language professionals might deal with this in the texts or speeches they are asked to recreate. From our conversations with experienced practitioners (see also Chapter 5) and from publications such as the *ITI Bulletin*, we perceived the potential need in a changing market for translators and interpreters to expand their skills portfolio and at the same time maximise the quality of their work. In this chapter we highlight a patchwork of transferable skills that you may already have or will be able to develop if you undertake the relevant CPD (continuing professional development). For this chapter, we asked various colleagues to tell us about their own experiences and suggest additional skills that our readers could acquire.

Project management and business skills

Kari Koonin FITI very much echoed our own views on the importance of target language writing skills and stressed the need for language professionals to adopt a business mindset from the outset and develop good communication skills "because we work primarily in a B2B (Business-to-Business) environment". Dr Brigitte Scott endorsed this, saying, "Over the years I have perfected my project management skills (at scheduling, price negotiation, and invoicing) but there are now tools for that as well, which might be helpful for newcomers into the profession".

For anyone wishing to enhance their business management skills, various professional organisations offer online courses, such as the ITI's *Setting Up as a Freelance Translator* and *Advancing Your Freelance Translation Career*. A review of the first by Rosie Dymond and a joint review of the second course by four recent students were featured in the *ITI Bulletin* in May–June 2020 and November–December 2020 respectively. The range of courses run by the CIoL likewise includes a one-day workshop on *Setting Up as a Freelance Translator: Pricing Strategies and Negotiation Skills Workshop*.

DOI: 10.4324/9781003136903-5

Auditing your current skills

Dr Hayley Harris made a very interesting point:

> Recommending transferable skills is a broad remit, as it depends to some extent on the translator's area of interest. However, one recommendation I would make is for a person to 'audit' their existing skills to identify what might be transferable. We are often more skilled than we realise and bringing this to the attention of others may enhance our value in their eyes.

If you do an audit of your skills as Hayley suggests, you will probably realise that through practising your craft you have become, almost imperceptibly, an excellent communicator. This may take the form of good public speaking skills, writing and editing skills, or even transcreation. In Chapter 4 of *Translation: A Guide to the Practice of Crafting Target Texts* (Cragie & Pattison 2020), we introduced readers to creative writing techniques, demonstrating how these can improve the quality of the translated product. In the present book we will look at the commercial aspects and applications of writing and editing, such as summary writing and abstracting. The exercise of these skills offers the additional benefit of enhancing the quality of the service that you can provide to clients, with the ultimate aim of moving up into the 'premium' bracket.

The premium market

In our experience, there appears to be a kind of symbiotic effect when translation skills interact with analytical and creative skills, making the end result greater than the sum of the individual parts. In an article entitled "The countdown's started", published in the *ITI Bulletin* November–December 2020, Chris Durban FITI reveals how you can move into the high end of the market. There is a bulk, a middle and a premium market, she explains. Those in the middle will need to train up if they are to flourish as the industry becomes saturated with "an influx of desperate newbies made redundant from other industries hard hit by the pandemic", who may well have a wider range of professional contacts than the average translator.

Chris explains that to move upmarket, you will need to upgrade your skills and become exceptionally good at what you do, which includes having perfectly honed writing skills. You will also need to become familiar with the set-up in the industries you want to target as a potential source of clients. You will then need to find ways of "making contact from the inside". All this is not something that can be achieved overnight and requires a great deal of effort and commitment, she stresses. You will need to come across as a highly experienced and competent professional who can provide "effective communication".

Paul Boothroyd MA, MITI comes to mind as a translator who has made a success of a communication-based approach, with his specialism in PR, automotive and management consulting.

Once a premium client has learned to trust their translator, he says, involvement could extend to transcreation of voice-overs for video material, revising English language material drawn up by non-native speakers in-house or working closely with PR agencies commissioned by the client to cover major events.

> Take the Tour de France, for example: a major client sponsors the Tour and employs a PR agency to provide day-by-day coverage in the form of short press releases produced very fast. As the translator, I'm expected to read up on the Tour in advance – in magazines such as *Cycling Weekly* – follow the Tour online or on TV, and in the process of translating, check that the press releases are factually correct (who won the day's stage, who was on the podium), as well as checking any geographical references and the spelling of the names of people and places. All on top of a specialist knowledge of the client's products.

One essential aspect of the relationship, Paul adds, is having the confidence to question what is put in front of you in the source language and the ability to rewrite what is not communicated clearly, without detracting from or falsifying the message. "Then you need the interpersonal skills to communicate any errors or necessary changes to the client without causing loss of face for any of the parties involved".

In order to become familiar with the jargon used in a particular industry, and identify its major players, we recommend reading the trade press in your source and target languages, much of which is available online. For the packaging industry in German-speaking countries, for instance, there is *Neue Verpackung* and for information on the Italian market, you could scan through *Rassegna Imballaggio*.

Genealogical/historical research

One example of how Hayley's suggestion might be implemented is in genealogical research. The ability to read handwritten letters and other documents written in the old Gothic script or printed in *Fraktur* is a skill that can be put to practical use when delving into a family's history or working on material that dates back two or three centuries. Another colleague, Claudia Strachan MA, who had learned to read this script as a student at school in Germany several years before, has developed this area of research into a specialism. Whilst on an internship for a London museum, she translated letters written by German soldiers in WWI. This helped her to gain useful experience and meanwhile she has worked almost entirely in this field. She told us in January 2021 that "it's going from strength to strength, I'm happy to say". Claudia translates private correspondence, diaries, memoirs and official documents in the old German handwriting. "Some projects break my heart, particularly if they are linked to the Holocaust, and the email exchanges with the clients are highly sensitive", she said. Other commissions are so fascinating that she could work through the night because she finds it hard to stop. Her favourite assignments featured letters sent from a famous painter to his son in a POW camp during WWI; the diary of a German resistance fighter at the end of WWII; the memoirs of an aristocrat in the 17th century; a superstitious letter of protection for a soldier in the 18th century; the diary of the first woman in her country who was granted a divorce on the grounds of domestic violence; and an extract from a University's minute book recording the lectures of a famous German theologist and philosopher.

Claudia explained that part of the challenge in this stimulating work was that

> All projects make me learn history all over again, providing me with the perspectives of contemporary witnesses. In some cases, their education has been affected by poverty or specific circumstances and their spellings are very random. That's where another transferable skill comes in: having marked students' work for many years as a teacher, I learned to read the unreadable and it still helps me to decipher words that I would otherwise not recognise. Examples are *Vamilye* for *Familie* (family), *fi* for *Vieh* (cattle), *geheurath* for *geheiratet* (married), and so on.

Another colleague we spoke to has also been learning how to do genealogical research. We believe that the ability to decipher and translate handwritten letters written in Russian (or any other language in which there is a considerable difference between the printed and handwritten forms), in combination with an interest in history, might provide a useful addition to the services that you can offer to clients.

Teaching

Most of our other respondents had applied their language skills by teaching in further or higher education or by acting as mentors to new recruits to their profession. Professional interpreter and university lecturer Zoé Brill Diderich thinks that "becoming an assessor for exams and teaching languages are good ways to use your skills and share your knowledge with others". She also suggests that interpreters enhance their voice skills. One quite unexpected new skill that Zoé acquired after losing some of her NHS interpreting work involved retraining to teach resuscitation! This was very scary at first, but she was asked to take on this work because she had a postgraduate lecturing qualification.

Teaching is one of three services that US-based translator Steph Kantorski has added to her repertoire in the last few years. (The other two were transcreation and copywriting). Steph said,

> ESL/EFL was my original career out of graduate school, a stint that lasted 12 years and ended in 2002-ish. I have three advanced students to whom I teach English pronunciation and grammar. I didn't seek a return to education, but rather it sought me 18 months ago when one of my students asked if I could help her with pronunciation and things sort of snowballed. I'm truly enjoying it and it's opening new doors for my students, who are finance professionals.

The added bonus is that having to revisit and explain the mechanics of her language has kicked her other skills into higher gear. "Instead of working from a place of linguistic intuition when writing, I can now see the nuts and bolts in my head more clearly. Full circle!"

Copywriting

Copywriting, Steph explained, "involves writing brand new copy in English based on a target and tone the client requests. These clients are either Francophone or Anglophone. For example, I copywrite product pages for BIC and Michelin (French) as well as Can-Am (English-Canadian)".

> This is a wild ride and it takes a lot of time to research the topic, play around with the tone/sonority/register, etc. I have to draw on every ounce of my 20+ years of wordsmithing to get the copy just right. I also love this service and am thinking of moving toward billing myself as a copywriter instead of a translator – especially given the direction in which the translation industry is moving.

We asked Steph how she came to add copywriting to the portfolio of services she offers. She explained that a translation agency she had been working with for almost eight years started branching out into non-translation services a few years previously. Since she had been doing some transcreation for BIC, a French manufacturer of disposable consumer products such as pens, lighters and razors, the agency asked her to do a few tests for new copywriting clients. "Those clients chose my submissions and one thing sort of led to another. The PMs at that agency know I'm always up for a creative or unusual project, so I guess I fit the profile for copywriting", she added.

How do you hone your writing skills in this specialist area? There are various short courses available online, such as those offered by City University London, by the London College of Communication and by the UK-based College of Media and Publishing (CMP). In *Netzblatt* Issue 124, February 2021 (the newsletter published by the ITI German Network), Dr Kate Sotejeff-Wilson MITI, describes the CPD she undertook with CMP, which gave her a good introduction to the basics in 20 lessons. Kate said, "you might not need an accredited copywriting qualification, but if you do, the CMP course is for you". "Its great strength is tutor support and constructive feedback", she added.

In Steph's case, she started a blog several years ago, featuring translations of historical French recipes and cultivated a solid online following, having been advised that this was the best way to find a publisher for a non-fiction work of this kind. She recommends that avenue, mainly as a way to practise and showcase your writing. Success may still be yet to come in the way she hoped but meanwhile she has been able to use her blog entries as samples of her work for prospective clients/agencies.

Transcreation

"As you probably know, **transcreation** is a hybrid of translation and copywriting", Steph Kantorski told us. She transcreated a website myparrotisrich.com, for example, which gives a very clear explanation of what transcreation involves. "The client gives me either a few notes on their product or a French text and I go to town transforming it into a relatively new and more culturally-appropriate text in English", she explained, adding

> I absolutely love doing these jobs, but clients neither seem to understand nor fully trust the process. It can make them nervous that I'll veer too far off their subject and they won't get what I did. I think the results tend to be way better in terms of truly localizing copy for a specific place or audience. Yet it takes additional skills that not all translators necessarily have. Or perhaps they need to have been translating for a very long time to trust themselves to really grasp this type of creative writing.

In "What's the difference between translation and transcreation?" published online in https://translatorstudio.co.uk/difference-between-translation-transcreation (accessed on 24.01.21), Gwenydd Jones explains, "Transcreation refers to creatively translating marketing materials, whereas translation has a much broader meaning. Translation is about producing an accurate and idiomatic rendering of the original text. Transcreation, on the other hand, involves translating with more artistic licence". In other words, transcreation is closely allied to copywriting. She adds that "Besides being a qualified, professional translator, a transcreator is a trained copywriter" and points out that transcreators have more leeway to edit their source texts, whereas a translator cannot add or remove any of the information content without express instructions from their client. As we understand it, transcreators aim to convey and transpose concepts to a different culture rather than directly translate carefully worded messages. In the May–June 2017 *ITI Bulletin*, Toby Bristow described an ITI workshop on "The Mysteries of Transcreation", run by Rik Grant of World Writers, who explained that "translation is seen more as a product, while transcreation is seen as a service".

When asked if they had any experience of transcreation, many of our colleagues echoed a comment made by Paul Boothroyd, "It's part and parcel of my everyday work" (one of the areas in which he works is PR). Brigitte Scott, for instance, has transcreated adverts and song texts and some of the texts she translates for photography books also border on transcreation. In addition, she has translated press releases and publicity material and produced German versions of a couple of cookbooks and other food-related texts. What she considers her biggest achievement was the English translation of a book on a garden through the seasons, which was well reviewed by the RHS (Royal Horticultural Society).

In a recent magazine article about an early Dutch cyclist, Nick Rosenthal worked with the original journalist to produce a fluent and highly readable English text. This involved reorganising some of the information into a slightly different order and fronting the piece with "Her career got off to a tricky start", although in the Dutch text this had appeared at the end of a list of setbacks. "It's all about the narrative", he explained. To illustrate the importance of applying your analytical skills to determine what the reader needs to know, Nick quoted the example of the habit that foreign journalists adopt of referring to a sporting celebrity, for instance, by a nickname such as 'der Rostocker' ('the guy from Rostock') to avoid repeating a name – in this case that of the cyclist André Greipel. The technique used in the German source text is known as **elegant variation**. A similar example Nick gave of how to contextualise references for an English-speaking reader was describing the location of a factory in Baden-Württemberg as being 'near Stuttgart'.

Transcreation-related activities that require competence in both writing and translation include scanning and summary writing. These usually involve reviewing information in foreign trade publications for clients who lack knowledge of the source language and producing summaries in English that highlight the client's main areas of interest. For this you need to think analytically and have an awareness of both detail and the whole picture, something which we have aimed to foster in this book by explaining how to identify the linguistic features of a source text and identify changes in usage.

Content marketing

One further area into which some translators have already diversified is 'content marketing', an activity defined by the Content Marketing Institute as "a strategic marketing approach focused on creating and distributing valuable, relevant, and consistent content to attract and retain a clearly defined audience — and, ultimately, to drive profitable customer action" (https://contentmarketinginstitute. com/what-is-content-marketing). Because it basically involves writing a story around a product or service, it provides a commercially viable outlet where wordsmiths can apply the creative writing skills they have developed in the exercise of their craft.

Steph Kantorski said, "Technically speaking, while I haven't offered content marketing as a service, I have translated a lot of copy that is ultimately used for this purpose".

We should also mention that it is worth taking the time to improve your marketing skills. A useful starting point is English-Swedish translator, localizer and transcreator Tess Whitty's podcast "*Marketing Tips for Translators*".

Writing abstracts and summaries

If you work with patents or translate scientific papers you may well be familiar with abstracts or have been asked to translate them. You may not have been asked to produce an abstract yourself unless you work in academic research. In a monolingual context, researchers and academics applying for funding grants or submitting articles to academic journals often have to supply an abstract of their proposal in the application form.

A client may need you to write a summary in your target language of a text or batch of documents that were first produced in your source language. A brief of this kind involves information transfer from one language to another but is argu-ably more akin to paraphrase than to translation itself. You may be asked to sift through and summarise archive material for academic researchers or genealogists, a task that involves a familiarity with archaic lexis and registers, such as 'Lutheran Protestant Consistory'. This term was used (with a gloss added by the translator) in a recent assignment to describe an administrative body governing church matters. Even in a summary, such a detail was important since the client needed to know who, or rather what kind of establishment had written these letters, which dated back to the 1820s.

One of our colleagues, Tim Morgan, told us that city lawyers had quite often asked for someone to go along to their offices and 'mine' a pile of foreign language documents so that they could retrieve information relevant to a particular case. Any summary the translator produced might then need to be certified in front of a notary public to attest to the accuracy of the information it contained. Of course, a translator undertaking this kind of work is likely to need a law degree or a quali-fication and/or experience in legal translation because they might not spot the significance of one particular word that could be crucial to the interpretation of the case. Another issue is how to quote for it – an hourly rate is probably the fairest method, but we do wonder how you decide how many hours you need or determine whether the speed at which you work is faster or slower than average!

One of the authors was trained to produce abstracts of articles written in English and other languages. The task was often preceded by two or three hours of scanning. In this case, scanning meant reading through a large batch of trade journals and newspapers in both English and all the languages in which she had a good reading knowledge to pick out research developments and market trends that the employer's subscribers could then be informed of in the company's internal news bulletins.

Abstracting is a skill that is not only useful in the marketplace; it also enables you to improve your comprehension of your source language or languages so that you can decode complex academic, business, legal, or scientific and technical texts. It helps you to enhance your logical thinking skills and grasp the line of argument that runs through it, rather than focusing too much on individual details. At the same time, your encoding skills in the target language will benefit from your greater understanding of the information content. Before the advent of free online machine translation tools allowed them to get a vague idea of what a foreign lan-guage text was about, clients concerned about the limitations of their budget would often ask for a summary of a longer text before commissioning a full trans-lation. This enabled them to pinpoint exactly which sections would be relevant to their particular project. Even now, a translator who can offer to provide a quick summary of a somewhat rambling report has a better chance of persuading the client to embrace a human rather than a machine translation option.

Summary writing is known to improve the translator's analytical and decoding skills. In *The Interpreter and Translator Trainer*, Bowker and McBride (2017: 259–279) demonstrate the use of monolingual summary writing in speed training for third year translation students on a BA Translation programme at the University of Ottawa.

In business too, the ability to sum up the key points in a report is a useful transferable skill. So how do you go about it?

- Look for the answers to the following questions: Who? What? Where? Why? When?

To produce an effective summary of a text, you first need to focus on what journalists call the five Ws. These were the most important facets of a news item, which ideally had to be covered in the first one or two paragraphs in case the article had to be cut so it would fit on the page. In the days before desktop publishing, this was done from the bottom upwards, so it was important not to leave the best bits to the end!

- Stick to the basic facts and remove all the trimmings. There is no need to provide background information to contextualise or gloss the text.
- Do not comment on the stance adopted by the author. The stylistic conventions for this genre preclude any mention of the author – an abstract should be complete in itself, like a mini-saga or piece of flash fiction, for instance.
- Do not add any additional information, however interesting or relevant it seems to you. But, do not be vague when it comes to the timescale. If a report written in 2021 says "this year", you need to be specific and refer to the actual year in question. "Last year" would be expressed as "2020" and "next year" as "2022". This is because a researcher may be reading the abstract five years later and will not know which year the statistics quoted refer to. The information needs to be as specific as possible so that it can be retrieved easily from an online database or archive.
- Apply the same rule to geographical locations that are implicit in the source text. After a reference to Fribourg, for instance, it would be reasonable to add 'Switzerland' and after Freiburg, an abstractor writing for a UK or US audience might well need to insert 'Germany'.
- Use a fairly formal and impersonal register to maintain objectivity.
- This usually means using the passive rather than the active voice of verbs, such as 'is described', 'are shown', 'is outlined', and so on. Other commonly used past participles include *featured, presented, set out, highlighted, explained, discussed, analysed,* and *reviewed.*
- Use the third person.

TASK 1: PRODUCING A SHORT ABSTRACT

Choose an article (in your source language) relevant to your research interests or specialism.
Try to identify the main theme or argument and select the essential specific details.
Write an abstract (up to 250 words) of this text in your target language.
To help you, the paragraph below features an abstract of Chapter 1 from *Translation: A Guide to the Practice of Crafting Target Texts.*

In what way has this exercise helped you to enhance:

a   your thinking skills?
b   your decoding skills?
c   your encoding skills (i.e. your ability to set out an argument in writing)?

Specimen abstract:

> Both writers and translators need to be aware of the role played in shaping a text by three perspectives: time, context and culture. The concept of *time* and how it is measured was considered by philosophers, literary theorists and writers, including Pamuk, Woolf, Mann, Proust, Butor, Robbe-Grillet and Priestley. In literature, time is represented within different frames of reference and concepts such as 'emplotment', which the philosopher Paul Ricoeur borrows from Aristotle, and non-linear narrative techniques create considerable challenges for the translator. *Context* can be considered both logistically and linguistically, so the translator's interpretation of a text is a complex process that is inherently subjective. The difficulty of producing valid and coherent theories of language eventually led to semiotics, the study of signs and symbols. *Culture* reflects the historical, geographical, linguistic and social setting. It can be material or non-material or both, making it difficult to transfer cultural references between different languages. The focus here is not only analytical; it is also practical and creative because translators are also writers. They each need to develop their own voice as a writer and explore time, context and culture from a writer's perspective before they can truly identify and recreate another writer's voice. (201 words)

Rewriting and editing

Rewriting and editing are some of the transferable skills that forward-looking translation and interpreting course providers are trying to include in future programmes (together with business and project management skills). As technology advances and machine translation becomes more widely used, newly qualified translators may struggle to find work. The key to success could well involve the ability to diversify and offer additional services. The working environment is becoming increasingly competitive as businesses and institutions struggle to survive the financial crisis, so one useful sideline that translators could provide is editing and checking the quality of documents written in their target language, such as CVs, company reports and applications for research funding. Even if the documents in question have been drafted in the writer's first language, which may not be the case in the global multilingual marketplace, they will often benefit from scrutiny by a second pair of eyes rather than merely by an online spellchecker or grammar checker.

There may be no linguistic or translation errors nor problems with formatting, but the text may just lack fluency because writers structure and express their thoughts differently depending on the language in which they are writing. Discourse conventions, that is, the techniques regularly adopted to discuss a subject either orally or in writing, not only vary over time, they also differ from culture to culture. This means that an argument presented by a French- or Spanish-speaking social scientist, for instance, might have a slightly more rigid structure than one put together by their American counterpart. Reporters from different cultures also present their ideas in a different way. In *Sixty Million Frenchmen can't be Wrong*, Canadians Nadeau and Barlow compare the rhetorical styles adopted by French and Anglo-American journalists. They explain that French style appears to be based on the "Thesis, Antithesis and Synthesis" model that is taught in French schools, which place a strong emphasis on teaching philosophy and Cartesian logic (2003: 180–181).

When editing or rewriting academic papers, business reports or presentations by non-native speakers of your first language, the key factors to consider reflect many of the points highlighted in our model. You will need to look at these criteria from a different angle, asking yourself different questions and addressing them in a different order perhaps. For instance, you may have to consider:

Purpose/use/brief: what does the client expect me to do?

The client may just want you to ensure that the text written in your target language is grammatically correct, that no typos involving homophones have crept past the spellchecker, and that the punctuation complies with the standard rules (i.e. to produce a light edit).

Alternatively, they may want you to iron out all the less obvious infelicities that detract from the overall quality of the text as an authentic piece of writing (i.e. produce a full edit). This will include ensuring that the theme of the text is expressed clearly and coherently.

PAUSE FOR THOUGHT 1: BE ALERT FOR ERRORS

We recently learned a new French term from a client when we queried a suspected typing error or *typo*. She referred to this colloquially as a *coquille*.

If you work out of a different source language, how do clients from your source culture refer to typos?

If you plan to edit English texts, compile a list of the most commonly confused or misspelt words or homophones, such as *lead* (a heavy metal) and *led* (the past tense of the verb *to lead*) and add them to your glossary or mental checklist.

Interpreters, for example, need to watch out for *prostrate* (meaning *supine, lying in a horizontal position*) and *prostate* (often used to describe a form of cancer that affects men).

If you edit texts written in another language, make a list of frequently occurring errors in that language.

Subject/theme: how clearly does this come across?

Assuming that you are engaged in a full edit, is the 'Thesis, Antithesis and Synthesis' model adopted by the author appropriate or is some restructuring needed? The job you are doing in the latter case may be approaching transcreation even though you may not have seen a source language version of the text (assuming that one ever existed). This leads us to examine a further criterion – the target readership. If you see any evidence of new attitudes in the text, will they be known to the intended audience or do you need to add some kind of exegesis or explanation?

Purpose and brief

Is the text for publication, for information or is it a paper to be delivered at a conference? A text for publication will require a fuller edit than one purely needed to disseminate new information of an ephemeral nature, such as a weekly e-bulletin for a business or for a leisure facility, such as a sports club. If the newsletter is aimed at potential investors in a biotech business, a higher level of accuracy and style will be expected than for members of a supporters' association who want to know the latest rules regarding social mixing. If you are revising the language used in an academic paper that is initially going to be delivered orally to an audience from all over the world, it needs to be made as clear and simple as possible so that everyone can follow the argument.

Genre/format

If you have been asked to produce a camera-ready text or a 'turnkey' website, has the writer observed the latest formatting conventions prevalent in the target culture? Does anything need updating? Is there the right amount of white space and a good balance between text and images? Did you check the captions to the graphics? As a reviser, it is easy to miss a typo or awkward rendering if it appears in a smaller font under a diagram or graph or in a footnote to an academic paper or in a list of references.

The target readership

Do you know who is likely to read this text? Are the potential readers medics, engineers, social scientists, market analysts or actuaries? What is their language of habitual use – a) privately and b) in their work?

If you have been asked to do a full edit, you will need to consider whether the text targets a specialist or non-specialist audience and check that any idiomatic expressions will be familiar to an international readership. You might also want to decide whether you should use a more 'global' register.

Context/culture: how do they affect lexis and register?

Education, public health, and the social sciences are fields in which the culture of the social sphere advocates compliance with the latest social conventions so you may need to check that these have been observed. The social culture may well dictate the author's choice of lexis and register, but you may have to ensure that the language is appropriate and up to date. New and repurposed terms that translators and revisers/editors working with English social science texts in the context of ethics will have had to assimilate into their everyday lexicon include: *actors; charters of secularism; consequentialist; cultural competence; deontologically-minded; equal marriage; ethnography; frames of reference; normative international relations; post-liberal; and prioritisation decisions.*

Sometimes a term may seem unfamiliar to you, but it may be perfectly acceptable in the context. If in doubt, check it out! A further example we encountered recently is 'Catholic pillar'. This has a rather specific meaning in relation to the religious bodies in Belgium and the Netherlands so it would be incorrect for a reviser to replace it with a synonym. Moreover, in the social sciences, researchers will frequently introduce new labels to describe new concepts, such as, for example, 'pluralist secularism', which describes a school of thought that takes a fresh look at the relationship between the state and religion.

If the text is aimed at an international global audience, how will this affect the terminology you select? A multilingual audience may not be familiar with new terminology or with new norms for gender inclusivity and you may need to ensure that these are made clear within the context. An example of this would be to avoid using *he* (or *she*) as a default pronoun, and opt for *they* instead, which was a recommendation a reviser had to make to the editor of a social science book intended for a global readership.

TASK 2

Pick five of the above terms used in ethics and try to find texts that illustrate or explain their meaning.

If you translate out of English, can you identify possible target language equivalents of these terms?

If you translate out of French, what other renderings for *pilier* might work in other social science contexts?

Viewpoint

Do you detect any conscious or unconscious bias in the text you are editing? If you do, how should you deal with this? To what extent is this within your remit? It is probably wise to point this out tactfully to your client.

Meaning

Is there any ambiguity in the text that you need to iron out? Has the author used any words or phrases that have acquired a new meaning (e.g. *actor*)?

PAUSE FOR THOUGHT 2: STYLE CHECK LIST FOR REVISERS

This list of potential sources of error includes infelicities found in English texts written by speakers of other languages and also seen in students' translations. Things to look out for are, for example:

Colons: The use and function of the colon varies from language to language. It may need to be deleted from the English sentence and replaced by 'that is' or 'including'.

Contractions: In formal academic writing it is not advisable to use contracted forms such as *isn't* or *doesn't*, which are considered too informal. When editing a text, you may need to write these out in full.

Dashes and em rules: These are used (in pairs) rather more often in English than in some other languages to place additional information in parentheses. In UK English we tend to use brackets.

Ellipsis: The use of three dots … to indicate a missing word or words is less common in English than in other languages. They can be used to suggest the continuation of a list like 'and so on' or to introduce an element of speculation, such as 'who knows what will happen next?' or 'the future will tell'.

Incorrect use of conjunctions such as, *however. However* is not a coordinating conjunction so it is not interchangeable with *but* and should not be used to join two clauses together.

Missing definite or indefinite articles/incorrectly used articles (the, a, an). This is a common error in texts produced by speakers of Slavic languages.

Neologisms (such as *Djane* for a female DJ): will the target audience be familiar with these terms or do you need to make them clear in the context?

Nominalisation (use of noun-based structures): a verbal noun or gerund may need to be replaced with a verbal structure such as a relative clause.

Phrasal verbs: Consider whether it might be better to use a more formal verb derived from Latin or Greek (e.g. *separate* rather than *split up*).

Tenses: If you spot a conditional tense (such as *would be*) being used where there is no actual condition involved, this may be because the verb refers to a theory, allegation or rumour. In English we would simply use the present tense (*is*).

Remember that in many cases a present continuous tense conveys the meaning more clearly when an ongoing process is being described. So, instead of *are mobilised*, you could use *are being mobilised*.

Writing a commentary or a preface and annotations

Commentary writing is a skill often required on postgraduate translation courses and for some professional examinations so that translators can rationalise their choices and demonstrate their critical awareness. For what some universities refer to as an extended translation, students may be asked to present a brief overview analysing the linguistic features of the source text and explaining how they plan to approach it. They then need to identify translation challenges and explain the strategy they adopted to solve these problems. In *Translation: A Guide to the Practice of Crafting Target Texts* (Cragie & Pattison 2020), the sample translations were accompanied by annotations describing an overall translation strategy (known as the macro strategy) adopted for the text as a whole, which took into account the genre, purpose and potential readership of the source and target texts, for example. Where possible, we identified a parallel text that could be used as a model for the translation. This was followed by a set of five or six micro strategies addressing individual issues involving lexis, register, use of tenses, ambiguity, cultural gaps, stylistic features such as irony, use of metaphor, idiomatic expressions, and lack of equivalent terms in the source language, and problems with cohesion and coherence.

Typical micro strategies that can be highlighted in annotations include:

- expansion (making information that is implicit more explicit to bridge the cultural gap);
- modulation (shifting the perspective from a glass that is half-empty to a glass that is half-full or vice versa.);
- restructuring the syntax to improve coherence and cohesion; or
- transposition (replacing nouns with verbal structures or changing active to passive or vice versa.).

The aim of such annotations is usually to demonstrate that you are aware of where the challenges lie and can justify the solutions you have chosen, using translation theory to evaluate or compare the relevant merits of alternative solutions. Competence at writing such a commentary is intended to prove that the translator can rationalise the translation process and think like a language professional.

TASK 3: IDENTIFYING CHALLENGES RELATED TO SOCIAL AND LINGUISTIC CHANGE

Read one or more of the texts in Chapter 2 or Chapter 3 and make a list of the types of translation challenge involved, such as neologisms, gender equality issues and sociocultural gaps.

What strategies could or did the translator adopt to solve the problem?

Can you think of an alternative strategy or solution?

Although you are not likely to have to write a commentary for most professional assignments, it is not unusual in a literary translation for the translator to write an Introduction, as Alec Hargreaves did in the case of *Shanty Town Kid*. He prefaces Naïma Wolf's and his translation of Azouz Begag's memoir with a brief account of the lives of migrant Algerian workers who settled in France. In his explanation of the origins of the term *Beur*, he says that it "had originally been coined in the 1970s by second-generation North Africans in the banlieues of Paris. It is generally considered to be a piece of *verlan* (back slang)". Hargreaves stresses Begag's desire to celebrate cultural diversity and "create a better understanding of France's North African minority by returning to an earlier period and presenting it through the often naive eyes of his childhood alter ego". He also discusses the translation challenges presented by "multiple linguistic registers" and considers the merits of potential solutions for rendering in English the mixture of French and Arabic slang that Begag uses (Wolf & Hargreaves 2007: xiv–xviii). In both the source and target texts, glossaries of Arabic terms are provided but the English version is more extensive since English-speaking readers would be familiar with fewer terms than their French counterparts.

Explaining your translation strategy by writing annotations is a useful exercise because it helps you to adopt good professional practice and provides you with the necessary tools to justify your translation choices to a client who thinks you should have adhered more closely to source text lexis or structures. You will become a more confident and competent translator and, if you work on academic papers or historical documents, you will be able to highlight ambiguities or possible omissions in the source text.

PAUSE FOR THOUGHT 3

If you are compiling a translator's note to make your reader or an academic client aware of neologisms you've spotted in the source text (such as the Spanish *lideresa* to describe a female leader) for instance, would you use the same register that you used in the commentary for your master's degree project?

In what circumstances would you consider such a note to be necessary?

Transferable skills for interpreters

During the pandemic, many language professionals have been using the spare time between assignments to undertake CPD in new areas. Zoé Brill Diderich advises the interpreting students she teaches to work on their translation skills as well, and pointed out, "There is no reason why an interpreter can't be a good translator. If you can strike a good balance between both, you can enjoy the benefits of using and developing your skills as a linguist".

Another interpreter, Amelia Naranjo-Romero MA DPSI RPSI MCIL MAPCI MAIT, who works from English into Spanish, advises colleagues "to learn other languages, to choose an area of specialisation and be prepared to diversify. A degree in translation is also very useful because it offers opportunities in many fields. Work hard on writing skills and definitely, IT skills are indispensable".

Frances Parkes, the voice coach we spoke to, suggested that interpreters could enhance their performance and acting skills, do further training in voice and speech and gain familiarity with computer technology. Barbara Werderitsch, a conference interpreter and translator working with Spanish, Catalan, German, French and English, has been enhancing her professional writing skills by writing marketing content to promote her profession.

TASK 4 (FOR INTERPRETERS IN PARTICULAR)

Read some of the posts on the language and linguistics blog written by phonetics expert Graham Pointon www.linguism.co.uk. Follow the links to find a recording of a radio or TV programme that highlights changes in English pronunciation or accents.

A particularly interesting programme featured in the blog is the Channel 5 documentary broadcast on 18 July 2020, "The Queen in her own words – literally" (https://www.my5.tv/the-queen-in-her-own-words).

Subtitling

Because subtitling involves technical as well as translation skills, and because subtitling courses are readily available at various academic institutions, we have included it in this chapter. Our discussions with practitioners highlighted the increased use of streaming platforms, such as Netflix, which was also mentioned in the ITI's latest trends e-book *Negotiating a New Path: Trends in Translation and Interpreting 2021*, and which could mean that there will be more work opportunities in this area. For translators interested in learning how to subtitle without having to first invest in any specialised software, UCL (University College London) offers a Basic Subtitling Skills course (in association with the CIoL), which lasts 11 weeks and is normally offered two to three times a year (see www.ciol.org.uk/cpd/other-workshops). A follow-up 11-week advanced course is also available, as is a course in cloud-based CAT tools.

We discussed the growth of subtitling with Dr Lindsay Bywood, author of a chapter entitled "Technology and audiovisual translation", which was published in *The Palgrave Handbook of Audiovisual Translation and Media Accessibility* in 2020, and which provides further information about the interaction between translation skills and technology used in subtitling and dubbing. Prior to this, Lindsay, and her colleague Kristijan Nikolić reviewed trends in subtitling and related areas in *Audiovisual Translation: The Road Ahead* (2021), analysing data collected from delegates at "Languages and the Media 11" in 2016 and "Languages and the Media 12" in 2018, with 100 and 60 participants respectively. One interesting finding was that "our participants felt that transferable skills, including project management, should be taught at university level". The issue of quality was also raised with regard to this sector.

Since these surveys of conference delegates were conducted, the industry has seen a surge in the demand for streaming content, both in English, and more recently in other languages, Lindsay said. The developing interest in non-English content means that the work prospects for English mother tongue subtitlers are much better than they were at the time of the first survey in 2016. However, it is not easy to make a living on subtitling alone if you have a family and a mortgage to support, so Lindsay advises her students to view it as part of a portfolio of services that they, as translators, could offer their clients. This is partly due to the perception of subtitling in the AV sector, where it is often seen as a hobby and the phenomenon of 'fan-subbing' has created a community where many film buffs are happy to subtitle their favourite films for free.

Payment in this sector is by the minute and an experienced subtitler is unlikely to achieve more than 80 minutes per day, Lindsay estimated. A newcomer would struggle to complete more than 30 minutes of completed film product in one day and all languages are paid at the same rate. The recommended Netflix rates are published online but subtitlers are not able to source their work directly from such a platform; it is supplied through third-party vendors or language-service providers who work only in the audiovisual sector. There is now also increased demand for subtitling of non-English content directly into another language other than English, such as from Korean into German, following the international success of the Korean film *Parasite*, for instance.

Awareness of foreign language content in the UK began with Scandinavian crime thrillers known as 'Nordic noir' on BBC4 and has now gained momentum since Channel 4 began screening international material at Walter Iuzzolino's instigation on its international slot known as *Walter Presents* in 2016. According to Elise Gallagher (www.thecustardtv.com/2018/04/interview-we-meet-man-behind-walter.html, last accessed on 17.12.20), Walter has "revolutionised how we watch television, and in so doing, created a new dawn for foreign language drama". Elise pointed out that the first foreign series he selected, *Deutschland 83*, still had "the highest ratings a foreign language show has ever received on British television".

More international content became available after Argentinian and other Latin American *telenovelas*, which had been popular for decades on that continent, reached a wider international audience and broadcasting networks in other countries (such as Germany, Portugal, Turkey and the US) began producing their own style of *telenovelas* (https://en.wikipedia.org/wiki/Telenovela, 17.12.20).

As for the tools used in this sector, Netflix has adopted the term 'assisted translation' to describe the combination of CAT tools, machine translation, and spelling and grammar checkers that its subtitlers use. There is also free software available, but it has its limitations. However, a lot of companies will now give cut-down versions of their proprietary software to freelancers working for them, so subtitlers can end up with several packages they need to use, Lindsay told us. There is cloud software and standalone software at a variety of pricing levels, so it will depend on the amount of work a freelancer undertakes. Most freelancers will buy a professional package such as WinCAPs, which just runs on a standard PC.

Research skills and compiling a glossary

Many of the activities discussed in this chapter highlight the role of research in preparing for any translation or interpreting assignment. Research skills are a transferable skill in their own right and you should definitely include these when you produce an audit of your own skill set. Experienced interpreters or translators preparing for assignments in a medical context will automatically go to their own trusted medical websites in both their source and target languages but how can newcomers to these professions check the reliability of the terminology and information listed on online resources?

One strategy is to look, for instance, at the final letters of the URL to see what kind of organisation it originates from. Information on how to evaluate details of domain suffixes such as '.ac' for academic institutions in the UK and '.edu' for those in the US can be found on various websites, such as www.wuth.nhs.uk/m edia/17995/helpsheet-no-4_evaluating-web-resources-v_4.pdf (a useful guide to web resources for NHS staff) and on library guides such as https://uscupstate.lib guides.com/c.php?g=257977&p=1721715.

Evaluating web resources has been essential since the advent of 'fake news'. Just because information appears on social media, it may not necessarily be correct. Long before the 'anti-vax lobby' gained momentum, misinformation about the safety of vaccines that circulated on social media had resulted, for instance, in a fall in vaccination rates leading to outbreaks of vaccine-preventable diseases, as highlighted by Susanna Keane in the April/May 2020 issue of *The Biologist*.

The activity below has been devised to replicate a typical research activity of the kind that an interpreter or translator might need to complete in the run-up to a professional assignment.

PAUSE FOR THOUGHT 4: BACKGROUND RESEARCH AND COMPILING A GLOSSARY ON CLIMATE CHANGE

From your own experience of working from or into a language other than English, how would you evaluate the reliability of website information that appears in that language? You are not likely to find any suffixes to help you but see if you can identify any other features that could indicate that the URL is reliable.

Let's assume that you are preparing for a conference interpreting assignment on climate change or are assisting an interpreter colleague with their research.

You therefore need to compile a bilingual or multilingual glossary of terminology commonly used to describe climate change.

Search for around half a dozen general articles on the subject in your source language and highlight around 25 key terms that appear more than once. We advise you to look at national newspapers, popular science journals and material produced by official institutions.

Do these terms appear in any of the multilingual glossaries that are available online, such as that published by the European Council (www.consilium. europa.eu/media/31085/climatechange_key-terms_bookmarks.pdf)?

> If not, can you locate suitable target language equivalents yourself?
>
> If these key terms do appear in an existing glossary, use other sources to check the terminology quoted has remained in current use.
>
> The glossary should include columns listing the sources of both source and target language terms.

This chapter has explored some of the transferable skills that you could consider adding to your portfolio as part of your ongoing CPD. It also provides a few pointers as to how you might proceed to acquire the skills that will enable you to thrive as a language professional and even move closer towards the premium end of the market.

The e-resources include a questionnaire that will help you plan your CPD for the next five years (see: www.routledge.com/9780367683252). Apart from adding new transferable skills, you might also consider developing a new specialism or enhancing your knowledge of an existing one through further study. This may well involve some research into areas that are of increasing importance, such as conservation and climate change. An article entitled "Weird and wonderful CPD" by Dean Evans, which appeared in the *ITI Bulletin* Sept–Oct 2020, would be a good starting point if you are looking for ideas regarding the more esoteric forms of CPD that some colleagues have completed.

It is also worth looking at CPD provisions for language professionals that are available from organisations based in your source language country. In Germany, for example, the *Online-Akademie für Übersetzen & Dolmetschen* provides a range of courses in specialist areas such as law and in interpreting, organised for the *Verein für Sprache und Kultur in Germersheim e.V.*

In the next chapter we review current and future trends and share intriguing insights from various colleagues regarding the inner workings of the sector and changes in working practices.

5

SECRETS OF PROFESSIONAL SUCCESS

Riding the waves of changing times

In this chapter we plan to tell you all you always wanted to know about working as a language professional but never liked to ask. As practising translators, we are aware that you have to know where to find the answers to terminology and subject-related issues that fall outside your comfort zone. In the old days, before the advent of the internet and social media, you were advised to go and talk to an expert. One of the authors started out as in-house translator with a large agrochemical company and if a translator was unable to solve a problem by consulting the resources in the company library, there were always agronomists and chemists who could help. The translation department did a lot of work for the patent agents on the floor below and they were always very helpful if you had a query.

Bearing this approach in mind, we talked to over 20 language professionals working in different sectors, countries and language pairs so we could gain a comprehensive view of technological and commercial developments in the industry. These colleagues provided us with case studies of their long-term careers and everyday working practices, explaining their views of current and future trends, and outlining their experiences with CAT tools, machine translation (MT) or remote interpreting.

In the course of the interviews, people recommended a number of valuable research resources and shared practical tips and personal insights that will be extremely helpful to both new and established language professionals. A full list of the questions we asked is available as an e-resource at www.routledge.com/9780367683252, together with some additional responses given in the interviews.

Changing trends in technology and working practices

The ITI e-book *Negotiating a New Path*, published online on 1 February 2021 and edited by Catherine Park, contains essays by various industry experts and academics

DOI: 10.4324/9781003136903-6

on trends in translation and interpreting in 2021. In the introduction, the editor points out that "The degree of negative versus neutral or positive work impacts of COVID has depended to a considerable degree on the markets that practitioners are serving". This view was confirmed by many of the colleagues we spoke to.

In our own interviews, conducted between October 2020 and January 2021, we were looking for individual insights from practitioners into how they and their profession had evolved and for information about future prospects for the sector. We were told several fascinating anecdotes that illustrate what the life of a language professional looks like in practice and how it has changed in recent years. Nick Rosenthal FITI, a former ITI Chair, said that one major development he had seen in thirty years in translation was in the availability of research resources. In the early 1980s, Nick had "a wonderful start" on a student placement with Intertext in East Berlin, where he used a manual Erika typewriter. Intertext had a library and librarians, where you would look through encyclopaedias to find out details such as how the Flying Scotsman took on water while moving. From a linguistic viewpoint, this placement represented an ideal learning opportunity for total immersion in German. English was not the first foreign language taught in the city at that time. Most students would have learned Russian at school, an influence which was borne out by the fact that in the local café, the Viennese cream-filled gateau *Sachertorte* was labelled 'Saschatorte'!

Kari Koonin FITI, who works from Afrikaans, Dutch and German into English, said: "Everything has changed: technology, computers, the advent of the internet, CAT tools, broadband, speech recognition, text-to-speech software and machine translation". Another colleague said that, in the early 1970s, some people at the European Commission were still writing out their work by hand, while others dictated their translations. Then there were the early word processors, which had non-standard commands that varied across the different models. When Kari started out as a freelance translator, she wrote to about 200 translation service providers in order to establish a viable client base, but now "You can go online and identify potential clients anywhere in the world". Of course, the downside to this is that "the whole world is your competitor." This can have an adverse effect on rates, which have stagnated recently according to most of the translators we spoke to. Some had even been asked to lower their rates.

After working in the UK for many years, Dr Brigitte Scott moved back to her native Austria in 1999 and retained some UK clients until the 2008 crash. Fortunately, she had started to look for local clients around this time, so these filled the gap created by the loss of all her British work providers. Through her teaching at the University of Innsbruck, she acquired contacts in academic circles, some of them in the geography department, which led to some fascinating assignments, such as working on the *Alpenatlas* and holding a salaried post as co-editor of a journal featuring research into and management of protected mountain areas.

In academic circles, she explained, researchers often have to calculate the translation costs in advance when they are putting together a research proposal and may need to spend the money awarded to them for the project by a certain deadline.

This means that it may be necessary to implement a prepayment system with the invoice for translation work being submitted towards the end of one tax year whereas the actual research may not appear in print until the following tax year! So, translators working in this field need good project management skills and have to keep detailed records of submission and publication dates.

A chartered linguist based in Italy, Zoe Adams-Green MIL, primarily takes on German to English technical translation jobs, but also works from French, Spanish and Italian. She has been freelancing for the past 15 years, but started her career as an in-house translator at SAP. She told us,

> There have been vast improvements in translation technology over the course of my career – some positive (improvements in terminology recognition, typeahead functions, for example) and some negative (movement towards pre-translation and machine translation, which is obviously client-driven through a desire to lower translation costs).

She added,

> Also, thank goodness payment by cheque is a thing of the past. I remember when my dogs chewed up a cheque for a couple of grand at the start of my career. I was completely unsure as to whether the client was obliged to replace it/would do so, and that was a very worrying moment! (They did replace it.)

In the article entitled "A world of change", compiled by Ros Schwartz, which appeared in the *ITI Bulletin* in Jan–Feb 2015, Paul Boothroyd MITI, an experienced German–English translator based in southern Germany, and colleagues from the Wordlink Forum, described some of the changes they had seen over a long career. On one occasion, Paul recalled, an urgent statement had to be sent by telex to a Greek translator 100 km away and the translation delivered by taxi because the telex machine was unable to deal with Greek characters!

Increasing commoditisation

Steph Kantorski MA, who provided a US perspective, said the changes she had seen in the course of her career were too many to count. She started out in the late 1990s

> before the Internet or even full-blown translation agencies were around. Since then, the industry has been ruthlessly commoditised and linguistic quality has suffered as a result, not to mention standards and expectations. Translation is a very misunderstood craft among the general public, and that has not really improved.

Tim Morgan, MA, ACA, a qualified chartered accountant, and a translator specialising in medical, legal and financial texts, who also teaches translation at master's level, has seen increasing reliance on machine translation and widespread use of translation software. He also felt that a more mechanistic approach to the process and a more superficial understanding of what "accuracy" means can lead to a reduction in quality. "Use of translation software can be an ideological choice, regardless of whether it is suitable", he commented, adding

> Within some agencies, there is an increasing lack of creativity or lateral thinking in the editing process because the checking of translation output is often performed by entry-level staff, whereas the ideal scenario would be for this to be done by more senior translators or revisers.

In the past, revisers would often write handwritten comments on translations they had reviewed and fax them back to the agency! The tendency in the current climate, Tim highlighted,

> is for the translator to become more conservative and less creative because if an editor doesn't understand why you've done something, they might assume that you've made a mistake. Yet it may be that they've failed to follow your reasoning because they are not integrating translation theory or are not considering the purpose of the communication in question.

Other colleagues pointed out that the market now tends to be dominated by four or five major operators, creating considerable pressure on prices. Of course, undercutting by businesses located in parts of the world with lower overheads may well be affecting agencies too. Translators who offer niche specialisms (as Kari does with horticulture, for example) and/or who work with several language pairs (as Tim does) are in a better position. Others, like Lucy Teasdale, a freelance translator of business and technology texts from French into English for some 20 years, found that turning down jobs when she was busy became more of a risk after the pandemic. There were also fewer run-of-the-mill business letters and emails to translate, which may be due to clients using free MT systems for this purpose.

Use of translation memory software tools

Lucy said the agencies she works with insist on translators using CAT tools. Another colleague told us that even with pro bono work, non-profit organisations such as Translators without Borders still require you to use a CAT tool, but we believe that they can provide this. The CAT tools most often mentioned were Trados and memoQ and most people we interviewed were happy to use memories that they themselves or trusted colleagues had produced but not always those created by unknown translators. In the US, Steph Kantorski has been using Trados both as a translator and a project manager since about 2004. Currently, she uses Trados 2017 Studio, a tool that she chose because "It's the leading industry application". She said that translation memory tools "are great for keeping content consistent across multiple translators and looking up obscure client-specific terms" but they can be highly-priced and "unnecessarily complex and contrived, as software goes."

Brigitte Scott said,

> In the late 1980s and 1990s I used dedicated CAT tools provided by my clients on their mainframe. I have tried out OmegaT but have never got such tools for myself to use on my PC. At first, I hesitated to spend so much money and later I had changed over to direct clients only (so was not required to use them) and editing became a substantial part of my work, as well as translating text in artistic photography books, and I did not think that CAT tools would have been very useful here.

She also uses Linguee a lot and finds it really useful to see the context in which a term is used.

Philippe Galinier MA is in a different situation since he has a contract to translate a wide range of material from English into French for a UK government department and he also teaches translation. The texts can vary from 'promotional' texts for UK candidates applying for international posts to official applications to international conventions and European Investigation Orders. The 'specialisation' element lies in customer knowledge and familiarity with text types. Philippe has been using CAT tools for at least ten years and finds that their main advantage is maintaining consistency. A quick click on his concordance icon helps him to ensure accuracy and allows a fast turnaround with subject matter in a field that is familiar to him. Although he started off using a Mac, he now uses a PC laptop, but the Mac still serves an important function as a second screen, on which he can keep the source text open, for instance. Due to the confidential nature of his work, he does not share his translation memories with anyone.

Paul Boothroyd MITI echoed Philippe's observation that using a translation memory tool "improves the consistency of the output, which with careful attention can be commensurate with quality. Satisfaction is more likely to be boosted by positive feedback". Other advantages of the tools mentioned by Paul were reduced typing effort and being able to identify source language material that clients had recycled from previous publications.

Emma Gledhill FITI embarked on a career in translation right on the cusp of a major development sparked by the wider availability of word processors and the beginnings of the World Wide Web. She bought Trados when it first became available and now also uses memoQ a lot. She sees the advantages of CAT tools as being the concordance function, which allows you to search for a specific term and retrieve all translated segments where it occurs, and enhanced consistency.

Kari has used CAT (computer-assisted translation) tools since roughly the mid-1990s, that is, for most of her career, graduating from IBM Translation Manager to Trados (Version 2.0 came on a set of floppy discs) and then to memoQ. She remembers doing a long, incredibly repetitive job for a direct client in the early 90s which I dictated to the audio typist I used. I gave repetitive chunks of text code names, like a kind of verbal Autotext, saying copy text A to here, text B to there, etc, and thinking how great it would be if there were some clever software that would do that for me!

Nick Rosenthal has even been using computer-assisted translation tools for slightly longer. By the time he returned to the UK from East Berlin, the early word processors were emerging, and he gained expertise with an Amstrad PCW, and with early modems, which led him to develop a specialism in computing. It gradually emerged that clients would pay a premium for speed and for quality of service. Soon, translation memory tools were starting to come out and he was well aware of the need for consistency. "With lots of technical stuff, you would think I've seen that word before, or you would keep coming across a repeated standard paragraph or phrase". Added to this, in the mid to late 90s, "IBM Translation Manager and Trados helped you to save manual labour".

In around 2013, Paul Boothroyd, an experienced German–English translator based in southern Germany, purchased memoQ, which had been recommended as translator-friendly by a respected colleague, when he realised that even in his chosen fields of PR, automotive and management consulting, which involve creative work, the level of repetition/reuse of previous material was increasing. He felt the need to get away from relying on an awareness of having "seen that somewhere before" and finding it via a desktop search, so he decided to invest in translation memory software.

Tim Morgan, unlike most of the other translators we spoke to, was not convinced of the commercial advantages of CAT tools for his work. He occasionally uses memoQ but does not currently have it installed. He added, "If work ever dries up I will buy it. It's straightforward, relatively inexpensive, and apparently compatible with other packages. It's also usable with multiple languages whereas some other software packages are more restrictive".

He explained, "Translation is essentially a communicative act. The process 'read–assimilate–re-express' is most effective, with the fewest distractions and interruptions. I translate best with just two elements on screen: source and target texts, presented as final products".

Tim kindly provided us with some valuable insights into what he considers to be the possible pitfalls and drawbacks of using CAT tools. They included the following points:

Visual placement of text in the document or database is an important clue in interpreting the communicative sense. There are ways to work around this, but it's obviously easier for the source text plus the layout to be combined, as they are in an ordinary document or display, rather than having to flip back and forth between multiple displays, screens or tabs. Lucy, another translator we spoke to, had a similar impression: "when translating in segments, you don't write as well and you follow the source text far too much", she said.

During the two years that he used a CAT tool regularly, Tim found he would spend a lot of time trying to figure out how to fix bugs and problems, such as segmenting and formatting errors. This involved looking on websites, talking to clients, seeking other help, applying manual fixes and workarounds, and experiencing delays in order to produce output which, in MS Word, simply requires typing out the translation. He added that it was never easy to work with "rips from PDFs because the text is usually full of errors, segments are usually mis-chunked", and the errors were then perpetuated when input back into translation memories.

Another of Tim's concerns was "ensuring a consistent authorial voice". This is

> taken care of largely automatically if you translate something from scratch, but if you're assembling a text like a jigsaw puzzle, voice has to be manually har-monised as an extra stage. A writer will have a number of hallmark stylistic characteristics, e.g. preferred syntactical structures, discourse markers, and these help the reader to navigate through the text. It's very common for whole chunks of text offered by the software to be plausible renderings of particular passages but to jar with the rest of the translation: yes, the translation is "authorised" by the client by having been approved in the form of a previous translation. However, the client obviously did not authorise the renderings in this new context.

The question also arises as to how essential terminological consistency is. The costs can be disproportionate. He pointed out that "client authorisation" of translations is dubious. "I've often been given glossaries or translations 'approved by the client' which proved partly useful but partly incorrect. Having to justify deviations in these cases is also very inefficient".

When Tim bases his translations on previous translations of his own, he often discovers that it takes longer to edit previous jobs than it would have done to translate the material from scratch: having software automatically fill in part of the translation often does not reduce the time it takes.

One of the problems as he sees it is that some agencies seem to view consistency with unrelated translations for the same client as an "ideological" parameter of a successful translation, regardless of the cost in terms of the effectiveness of the text itself as a communicative act or the efficiency of the process.

He added that editing translations produced by others using CAT tools could be far more time-consuming than editing ordinary translations because the terminol-ogy and phraseology were generally less consistent than in ordinary translations, despite the software's prompts, precisely because that translation memory is often not harmonised for phraseology and terminology. Translators either do not or are not given the chance to revise the translation at text level, taking into account the impact of the final text on the reader. In other words, over-reliance on the system rather than on their own minds could mean that translators fail to activate higher-level mental routines.

Another colleague pointed out that it was easy to lose track of the whole picture since what works at segment level doesn't necessarily work at text level. There could also be a problem with the use of elegant variation in translations out of the Romance languages, said a semi-retired translator we spoke to. One example would be in a text where the Italian equivalents for 'wall' and 'partition' were used as synonyms, so it was not clear whether the author was referring to the same thing or to two different things.

Machine translation

Our colleagues made it clear that machine translation is a useful companion to the translator's own translation memories but should not be considered as an alternative because it is essentially a quite different thing. Translation memory is an environment where you have all your existing translations to return to, and MT is an adjunct. Most people agreed that the quality of machine translation has improved tremendously and now most of the output is usable after good post-editing by a human translator. "Human communication needs an expert human eye to pick up the nuances", Kari said. "For manuals and general standard business texts MT is proving popular". "It can be useful," she explained, "because such texts are generally written in a fairly straightforward style that MT can handle relatively well, although some human intervention is still required to check the output". Kari uses MT mainly for reference or to suggest alternative renderings and to speed up some simpler texts. She has a paid DeepL account, which is a plug-in to her Memoq system.

Machine translation sometimes comes in useful, Lucy said,

> when the output makes you reconsider the standard way you translate certain things, so that you don't get stuck in a rut. For lists of names, countries, etc, using an MT system such as DeepL can save time and typing effort.

Nick has watched machine translation evolve over many years. It works well "when supported first by translation memories of your own work and second by a combination of TMs of your own and of respected colleagues". He stressed that "For me it comes back to the intellectual skills set" – the ability to ask, and to question whether we would use the passive voice in English as often as they do in a German text. "East Germany taught me to think carefully about who is saying something and why." One drawback of machine translation is that it is "not good on gender neutrality", whereas a human translator will usually write 'they' and 'their', instead of 'he' and 'his'.

Machine translation is suited to some languages more than others, adds Tim, an exceptionally talented polyglot who works from German, Swedish, Danish, Norwegian, Dutch/Flemish, Polish, Russian, Slovene, Croatian/Serbian/Bosnian/ Montenegrin and occasionally French. Such systems can parse the syntax well with Scandinavian languages, for instance, but there are issues with Slavic languages. "Slovene generates real problems", he added.

Administrative and legal Slovene often favours very long sentences and there is lots of embedding, with verbs being split so that the auxiliary and the past participle can be ten lines apart. An MT system cannot cope with this at all, and document recognition doesn't work well with languages like this that have a lot of diacritic marks. Even Norwegian can be tricky sometimes because of "auxiliary dropping" but Swedish and Danish are more straightforward.

Steph highlighted another application of DeepL, which she very occasionally uses to check her French when writing to a client. However, she does not use it for actual content in her work. She is concerned that MT may influence less experienced translators negatively because they might take it as gospel (barring any glaring errors) and points out that her reaction to MT is usually not to trust it, mainly because it lacks the benefit of context, style/syntax and regionalisms.

Paul has a DeepL Pro account and uses it occasionally "to provide wording when my mind goes blank or inspired phrasing won't come. It's like consulting a thesaurus".

Emma also has a DeepL Pro account and told us that neural machine translation "is very seductive and sounds very plausible" but is not always accurate or consistent, with the German *Kunde* being rendered as both "customer" and "client" within the same document. She pointed out that with the Pro version, you can upload entire documents. "Machine translation takes the drudgery out of the job", she said. "You can focus less on the mechanics of translation, which frees you up to be more creative. It can also help with the RSI (repetitive strain injury) issue."

A further point to consider with free machine translation engines involves **confidentiality**. Once you insert the ST into the online MT system, the system can record the ST. This could compromise confidentiality, as the source text may include the client's product names or staff names and suchlike. Emma, Kari and other colleagues stressed that, as a subscriber to the paid version of a service such as DeepL, there are guarantees to protect you from a data breach since your work is deleted as soon as you have finished translating it and the connection to the server is encrypted. The free version also offers this to a limited extent now, but you need the Pro version to take full advantage.

This contrasts with what Nick told us about data security in the 1990s, when a translator he met who was handling highly-sensitive material had a police-monitored alarm system, bars on the office windows and padlocks on the filing cabinets!

Machine translation post-editing

Many language service providers (LSPs) or translation agencies now offer what is known as MTPE (machine translation post-editing) to their clients and this area accounts for an increasing proportion of their work. At the same time, many freelance translators use machine translation for their own work and edit, or rather post-edit, it themselves. The background to this was explained at an ITI webinar in November 2020 entitled "All you need to know about post-editing", presented by

Dr Akiko Sakamoto from the University of Portsmouth. She said that a survey of EU translators found that recent advances meant that 66% of them now used MT on a daily basis. In her article entitled "Online assistance" in the March–April 2020 issue of *ITI Bulletin*, Akiko stressed the importance of trust between LSPs and translators, revealing that "LSPs tend to leave the matter to the translator's moral compass, saying trustworthy translators would never misuse MT".

Akiko explained that there are three basic types of architecture available in machine translation systems:

- rule-based MT (which emerged after WWII; a crude analogy of this is a computer with a grammar book and a dictionary in it);
- statistical MT (or SMT, which appeared in the late 1980s; this analyses a bilingual corpus of data comprising existing translations and determines statistically how a new sentence will most probably be translated); and
- neural MT (which is still data-based but uses neural networks for machine learning with the aid of artificial intelligence).

The first artificial neural networks were created in 1959 at Stanford University and we have seen their use for machine learning often being mentioned in patents, but it was not till 2014 that a paper was published by KyungHyun Cho et al. (2020) on their use for machine translation (Source: https://arxiv.org/abs/1409.1259).

Editing by human translators is required because machines lack the world knowledge and understanding of cultural and social factors that experienced human practitioners acquire over a long career in the sector. Paul commented that his experience of post-editing was very limited, but his general impression was that "anything reworked from a less-than-brilliant source will likely prove inferior to a product created from scratch by bright (human) minds".

Both Tim and Lucy have experience of post-editing machine translations. Tim says he is in principle available for MTPE, where the quality of the source text is good, and the machine translation produces a text that requires sufficiently little editing for time to be saved in comparison with ordinary human translation. Lucy told us that, for such assignments, agencies pay around 50% of her normal translation rate but sometimes the hourly rate works out higher when the machine has done a good job. It can then take her less than half the time that it would to work from scratch.

Tim is less convinced of this. "I have seen some machine-translated material which is half-decent", he admits,

> but even then it can take as long to edit as human translation, and human translation can take as long to edit as it would have taken to translate the document from scratch. After all, understanding the text at word level all the way through to text level, technical research, terminological research, checking for completeness, omissions, and transcription errors, final high-level editing, and proofreading take largely the same time in editing jobs as in translation jobs. The only work spared the editor is the typing stage in the

middle of the process. If what is typed needs to be substantially reworked, even this time advantage is lost.

He added,

> Most machine-translated material I have been provided with for post-editing requires full reworking. This can take as long as translating it from scratch. This is particularly true if cohesion, coherence, consistency (of lexis, terminology and syntactical structures) and communicative impact are required across the text as a whole.

These comments were reinforced by what Akiko said at the webinar. Ideally, clients want experienced translators to undertake this work, but they are reluctant to do it. For those who want to use their creativity, fixing errors may not offer enough job satisfaction. She referred to a Japanese researcher, M. Yamada (2019), who found that less competent linguists were prone to miss serious errors. In 2017, the ISO published *Guideline 18587* to cover MTPE. It makes a distinction between full and light post-editing, with the latter being intended "to obtain a merely comprehensible text without any attempt to produce a product comparable to a product obtained by human translation" (www.iso.org/standard/62970.html, accessed on 25.11.20).

Rates for this work appear to be calculated as a percentage of the rate for a normal translation but there are arguments for charging an hourly rate, as is often done for other editing work, and best practice has yet to be established.

PAUSE FOR THOUGHT 1: POST-EDITING

Take a passage from a text that you translated for a recent assignment.
Make sure that this material is not confidential.
Then paste the source text into a free online neural machine translation package such as www.deepl.com/translator.
How does the MT product compare with your own work?
Can it select the correct collocation, avoid calques and steer clear of words that are rarely used outside online dictionaries?

Now paste your own translation into the MT system and back-translate it into the source language.
Compare the back-translation with the original.
What are the strengths and weaknesses of each?

Then try this with a text in a similar semi-specialist field but from a different source language. If possible, use a language where the word order is very different from English, such as German.
How do you rate the performance of the machine translation engine with this language pair?

Other tools

Kari uses speech recognition software (Dragon Naturally Speaking®) to dictate the bulk of her work, within her memoQ memory tool. She says it helps to improve the flow of a target text and to create natural links between ideas. She also recommends text-to-speech software, which she uses to check her work by listening as it is read back to her. As reading and listening involve two different parts of the brain, this gives you a fresh perspective on a text, so she advises newcomers to the profession to use this software themselves to check their work if they can, or even to read their translations aloud to themselves. We found that on recent versions of MS Word, text-to-speech (*Read Aloud*) is already available on the Review drop-down menu and the software will read even highly technical target texts back to you clearly and at the speed you choose.

Paul said he had tried Dragon Dictate, adding "it was working well but I was less content with the accuracy of my work. It was much faster but when you're being creative, speed can be counterproductive. I find that while typing I have time to rethink and rephrase". This comment was echoed by Steph, who added, "I found that I 'think' through my fingers better than hearing/speaking it." Emma encountered similar problems to Paul with accuracy when she used this speech recognition software several years ago.

We also asked the translators about templates. Kari does use these occasionally when asked to translate certificates and suchlike. She said, "Keeping past certificate and diploma translations in an easily accessible place means you have an instant set of useful templates available when you need them". Other colleagues have a few template documents with style sets for particular recurring streams of work and, like Kari, use their own templates for professional certificates and suchlike.

Microsoft Word has a very useful Autotext function which can be used to save entire documents as templates. In the late 1990s, one of the authors was introduced to Autotext in Geneva as a major time-saving tool for recurrent phrases or paragraphs and she wondered whether people were still using it. Tim was the only one to still do so constantly. For long contracts, with terms of art in the law, for instance, it can be very useful, he said, but he is not getting as many such documents as he used to and suspects that they may have migrated to the TM route. He explained, "I code source terms or target terms prefixed with underscore and a 1, 2, 3 or 4 letter acronym/initialism to reproduce terms quickly (e.g. _mss becomes Member States)".

Useful resources for research and revision

Because translation quality will remain key in an increasingly competitive market, we asked our respondents to suggest some useful reference material that might help readers to ensure that their work is of the best possible standard. For researching terminology and contexts in her specialist fields of agriculture and horticulture, Kari finds that international research organisations, such as the research institutes of

Wageningen University and Research, are a vital resource (www.wur.nl/en/Resea rch-Results/Research-Institutes.htm – versions of this site are available in Dutch, English, French and German).

Philippe recommends a Canadian proofreading tool known as 'Antidote' (available from www.antidote.info/en/buy/first-purchase). This grammar and spellchecker is available in both French and English and also provides definitions and possible synonyms. Such tools provide an extra layer of quality control for translators who cannot ask a colleague to proofread their work because of its confidential nature, he told us.

Most translators we spoke to were frequent users of corpora, such as Linguee, which help them to see other possible ways of rendering a phrase. IATE remains a popular resource for names and titles of institutions and other such 'concrete terms' (some colleagues still have fond memories of its predecessor Eurodicautom) but it does not always provide you with the answers you were looking for. Because Kari has horticultural and agricultural clients in Germany and the Netherlands, she regularly uses IATE to check EU agricultural terminology.

Other useful resources recommended by the professionals we consulted were the Canadian bilingual common law database Juriterm (www.juriterm.ca), and Termium (www.btb.termiumplus.gc.ca), which is also Canadian and covers Spanish and Portuguese as well as French and English. Sarah Gudgeon (see p. 120–22) mentioned referring to stylesheets and specialised texts in the related field so that she can adhere to the most commonly accepted terms.

Emma mentioned *Eur-Lex* (https://eur-lex.europa.eu/homepage.html), the official website of European Union law and other public documents of the European Union, published in 24 official languages of the EU. The Swiss Federal database TERMDAT is also useful if you need to check the wording of Swiss legislation (www.termdat.ch). It contains the terminology of Swiss law, public administration and the public sector in Switzerland's four national languages – German, French, Italian and Romansh – and in English. It can be accessed free of charge online.

In areas such as legal translation where dictionaries go out of date more slowly than in more technical fields, paper dictionaries and specialist guides for translators are still useful. Philippe recommends Frédéric Houbert's *Guide pratique de traduction juridique – anglais–français* (2005), which is not a dictionary but a guide that examines how to translate some of the key features of legal discourse, such as *doublons* – duplicate or tautologous expressions like *null and void* or *last law and testament* (www. dicoland.com/fr/guide-pratique-de-la-traduction-juridique-anglais-francais-4226).

He added, "Frédéric Houbert has another excellent legal translation dictionary, *Dictionnaire de terminologie juridique anglais–français*. I use it a lot and there is a brand-new expanded edition which I certainly will purchase: www.dicoland.com/fr/dictionna ire-de-terminologie-juridique-anglais-francais-2e-edition-2020-6314."

Another useful tool for those working from English into French is René Meertens 2021 *Guide anglais–français de la traduction*. This work sets out some of the problem English words that are not easy to render into French and suggests possible solutions.

Other very good resources for researching new terminology are e-groups and networks for translators and interpreters, which allow you to post queries online. Some groups may be restricted to members of the relevant professional associations whilst others are open to all those who have a Twitter or LinkedIn account. Most professionals are only too happy to discuss terminology issues and it is particularly useful when you can connect with people who are living in the source language culture and can keep you informed of the latest social and linguistic trends. For those working on texts related to the pandemic, a useful multilingual coronavirus glossary in English, French, Dutch, German, Polish, Russian and Spanish has been compiled by the *Bundessprachenamt* and can be accessed online by members of the public at https://termcoord.eu/2020/08/bundessprachenamt-coronavirus-glossary/.

For information on neologisms in German, a useful account of *Internet lexicography at the Leibniz-Institute for the German Language* by Engelberg, S. et al. (2020) can be found at https://kln.lexicala.com/kln28/ids/.

The importance of intellectual skills

Nowadays, Nick like most people, has immediate recourse to Google instead of encyclopaedias for background information, but the same intellectual process is still involved. "You need to understand a process properly and find the way to express it clearly", he explained. Tim pointed out,

> Most of the work I do requires the translator to be fully on top of the material conceptually and to produce single communicative acts: coherence, cohesion and consistency within the document itself are far more important than consistency with other or previous texts, which may or may not be related.

For a translator working with balance sheets and accounts as Tim does, a lot of 'human override' of the lexis and syntax of the source text is needed in order to produce clean and simple communication in English. Financial accounts should never be translated automatically, he says,

> because what category headings denote will vary hugely from one set to another. I personally would not want a non-accountant to produce financial accounts. The financial understanding necessary to produce a set of accounts with terminology that accurately conveys the real content of each item is simply not accessible to non-accountants. This also cannot be automated. I don't reuse my own translations for financial statements across different companies for this very reason: the lexical set (e.g. how fixed assets break down into different categories) needs to be reconsidered from scratch every single time.

On a similar note, Paul highlighted the importance of context, pointing out that a single phrase can call for very different translation solutions in a manual, press release or CEO's letter.

Specialisms

Specialist areas evolve according to a translator's expert knowledge (of finance in Tim's case) and their passions (in Nick's case, cycling). "It all comes back to the things you love", Nick said. His experience of contributing regularly to a cycling journal led to his being commissioned to translate press releases for a German component manufacturer who was sponsoring parts of the Tour de France. The work had a very fast turnaround because the news from the race was hot from the press. Nick's knowledge and understanding of the sport meant that the client allowed him a free hand – quite an act of trust considering that they used the English text as a basis for translations into many other languages. He has now been compiling a French–English cycling glossary, which he updates on Twitter (@nickrosenthal), constantly adding the latest cycling jargon. A lifetime spent tinkering with bikes ("it's all about power transmission, which puts you on the road for understanding machine tools") sparked an interest in high-tech engineering, which then evolved into a further specialist area.

Paul works in similar fields, such as PR, automotive and management consulting, where he contributes to style guides or term lists maintained by his principal business clients.

After gaining his master's degree at the University of Westminster, Philippe started getting work in the fields of international development and relations and humanitarian aid, and this continued for several years, which is how he gained a knowledge of these areas.

Horticulture and agriculture have always been a keen interest for Kari, whose continuing professional development (CPD) activities include studying for a diploma in the former. The skills she has learned have also come in very useful in her own garden. Commercial horticulture was also a wise choice of specialist field given that people will always need food and growers will need to produce it! Her translation work in this field has therefore continued despite the pandemic.

Quality assurance: a key to success

When Nick took what his friends thought was "a very brave step" and set up a translation company in 1986, his initial plan was not to translate, but just to run the business. (He modestly claimed that it was not a great risk because he was living in a rented bedsit without any family or mortgage commitments, so there was nothing to lose.) It soon became clear that clients valued quality and were willing to pay a premium for it. At the time, the standard of bought-in translations was very variable, with some professionals lacking good target language writing skills. This echoed our own experiences around fifteen years earlier when one of us was involved in outsourcing translations from English into various languages for information relating to a new asthma drug. She and a senior colleague were a bit doubtful of the quality of a German translation and visited the agency in person, only to discover that the job had been completed by one of the secretarial staff, who was not a qualified or experienced medical translator.

This explains why accreditation by a professional body such as the ITI, CIoL, ATA, SFT, BDÜ or another of the over 100 national organisations that are affiliated with the FIT (*Fédération Internationale des Traducteurs*/International Federation of Translators) is so important and ensures that the work provided is of optimum quality. Nick and other translators we talked to had joined one of these at an early stage in their careers.

Nick was determined to ensure that his company provided their clients with excellent work. For the next two years, he worked as a freelance alongside running his own business, taking only four days off during this time. A traineeship as a management accountant for Unilever after graduation had provided him with some management know-how. He picked up clients from that field, including various Swiss universities, and with a colleague he translated a 600-page MBA-level project management handbook.

In order to maintain the quality and consistency of the work his company delivered, he paid for training and accommodation for ten translators attending a course at Trados UK. This helped him to build a successful model for his team, who were translating manuals for fax machines and suchlike into five or six languages. The next stage, in 2008, was the development of a shared translation memory system on the company's secure server, updated in real time. Nick tries to avoid splitting jobs but, for parallel-type related jobs, the shared system enhances overall quality and consistency.

So as to ensure that the company's translation memories reflect current terminology and linguistic usage, older memories from 30 years ago had to be deleted because of changes in the way we express things. Various colleagues endorsed Nick's view that translation memories used badly and containing input from up to 50 different translators with no quality control do not represent effective use of TM.

The in-between stage involving corpora such as Linguee is often overlooked, Nick added.

> Some translators are too focused on the word rather than the context. With Linguee you can click on uses and get more contextual information and see which is the good, the bad and the ugly. In other words, it stimulates the neurons. Of course, you need to look at the source of the entry and check the URL that it originated from.

Another translator commented that the advantage of Linguee is that it provides keywords in context.

To maintain very high levels of data security, you can use a private machine translation engine, such as SLATE Desktop[TM] or another private system. This allows you to input the TM from a long-standing client and produce an MT engine that's specific to that client. Then you can do a translation in memoQ, for instance, and line it up with Slate.

Current trends in the translation sector

Most of the translators we spoke to did not appear to have been badly affected by the pandemic although one said that it had made things even worse and another commented that translators working in the hospitality and tourism sector had been badly affected. Two or three people said there had been fewer inquiries from new clients. All our colleagues agreed that there will still be a role for human translators in the foreseeable future. "The day may come when I will sit back with a cup of coffee and a newspaper and the computer under my guidance will translate a million words, but we're not quite on the cusp of this yet", Nick mused. There is change afoot, though.

> When we took our car to be serviced 30 years ago – the mechanic would do it by ear, by listening to the engine to see what was wrong. Now they just plug it into an automated diagnostic system, but if I were to do that, I could end up ruining the engine. You need the expertise of the person overseeing the diagnosis. As with an experienced mechanic, the expertise of an experienced professional translator is still needed. Highly skilled translators will see a future.

Commenting in January 2021 on her personal impressions of how recent events had affected her workflow, Dr Hayley Harris told us, "There are many factors potentially affecting workflow, particularly including the increase in machine translation, Brexit and the pandemic. Whilst it is difficult to unpick the effects of these individual events, generally, my workflow has slowed in recent months". Asked about changes that she had experienced over her career of 19 years, Hayley explained: "I don't propose any of these comments to be hard facts and they are not substantiated by research. They are merely my personal feelings and perceptions and not representative of the general population". She feels that the overarching trends across the translation business include "an increasing drive for lower (or at least static) rates, deprofessionalisation of the translator's status and a preference for low price and high speed over quality – although quality becomes an acute issue when it isn't there!"

California-based Steph Kantorski was likewise concerned about the threat from artificial intelligence (AI). She said,

> As long as quality expectations keep decreasing, so will the role of human translators. Not only will we only be used to check what machines spit out, but the better the machines get because of that human tweaking, the further diminished our role will be. Human translation will eventually probably become a "specialty niche" for "brain-written" texts, like craft beer or cheese. There will be "purists" and "AI-free service providers" (this is already becoming apparent).

This translator drew a parallel with what happened in architecture in the 1990s:

> My mother went to architecture school in the late 1970s/early 1980s before AutoCAD. She never warmed up to computerized design and continued doing all her drawings by hand until she retired this year. She wound up catering to an upscale clientele who could afford her custom hand-done plans (which the builders always preferred). If she needed digital renderings or calculations for a specific purpose, she would hire a younger architect.

Sarah Gudgeon was more optimistic, "Personally, I feel that technology will only ever work in tandem with human translators; the issues of context and localisation require a certain sensitivity that computers don't possess".

Zoe Adams Green added,

> I think it will be a good couple of decades before machine translation can achieve anything like the quality of translation that a good translator can achieve. Those more likely to be priced out of the market by MT are the lower-earning, unqualified translators who translate on the side, or to get themselves through university, rather than professionals, in my opinion. Having said that, I'm future-proofed because I'm also a trained technical writer, and I'm taking courses to enable a swift change of direction to become a genetic genealogist if need be. Those are just contingency measures, though. At present, I don't feel threatened. In the long term, it's almost certain that – at some point – artificial intelligence will be such that practically perfect translations can be produced at the touch of a button. But we're not there yet.

Emma Gledhill said, "The machines are already here. We need to reposition ourselves."

From Germany, Paul Boothroyd commented,

> Let's say I would not like to now be entering the profession from university. I see a rapid advance in MT and a surge in demand for post-editing. Plus, further concentration of the industry as a small number of very large players pitch to and acquire the major corporate accounts by offering all-subjects-all-languages at low to very low rates, leading to a poorly paid freelancer market.

Tim's advice to new translators was: "Ensure that the presentation looks as professional as possible – excellence at the 'cosmetic stuff' will give you an edge". He added, "There are enough good agencies out there, so stick with them. Don't mess around with the lower end of the market". His love of and skill at formatting and layout resulted in regular commissions from agencies to "fix mangled material". He also produces visually identical translations as standard.

Concern was expressed by one translator about the dire situation regarding the teaching of modern foreign languages in the UK. This could result in fewer native speakers of English working as translators and being replaced by L2 translators, particularly in the case of languages like Romanian or Hungarian, perhaps. This colleague wondered whether MA graduates with English mother tongue do actually end up becoming translators. Sarah Gudgeon, who teaches ESL in Italy, told us "Some of my university students who would like to go into this field (translation) are quite worried about the influence of technology on the role of and need for human translators". However, there are mentoring schemes run by professional bodies (such as individual ITI networks) to help new entrants to the profession get established.

Views on the translation market from outside the UK

Emma Gledhill FITI is based in the Romansh-speaking part of Switzerland but spends several weeks every summer in Greece, where she skippers yachts and teaches sailing. Just before lockdown, she was offered a 'corporate gig' on a part-time basis, which was ideal because her freelance work had declined over the previous nine years, due to fluctuations of 30–40% in exchange rates with the eurozone. By late 2020, it was not financially viable for her to work with UK clients and was barely viable with eurozone clients. "The big corporates here tend to want to work with agencies that can offer a one-stop shop and SMEs run on a shoestring", she told us.

Based in Austria, Dr Brigitte Scott translates between German and English in both directions. She used to work on user interface texts for IT companies, then branched out into product marketing and internal corporation journals, later editing academic papers in English written by non-native speakers, mainly in mountain research (glaciology, protected areas) and political science (migration). She added, "In recent years I have also worked regularly with a photography publisher on unusual coffee-table books on a wide range of themes, from the Spanish Riding School to women victims of acid attacks".

The pandemic has hardly affected Brigitte's workflow. She always gets her work via email or download and the academics whose work she edits kept on writing when they were working from home. One change she had noticed was "The publisher is publishing less this year (2020) but I have cut back on the work I am doing for him since I semi-retired in 2017". With regard to the future, she thought,

> Translation will continue to be needed but it will be more difficult for young translators to establish themselves. They have to acquire and use the tools and will have to be careful not to go too far down the road of volume over everything because that makes for soulless work.

From Italy, Sarah Gudgeon said, "My love of the written word and my language skills means that I fell into doing IT:ENG translation work alongside my key roles" (as a journalist and English teacher). Her translation work has not been affected by the pandemic since

It's never been my main source of income but over the years I have done IT and business translation work for private clients as well as tourism texts for an agency. I have also done a couple of non-fiction books with a more experienced, qualified friend and colleague.

She decided to do an online translation course purely for CPD and "to feel more confident in my skills if and when I undertake more projects. I am working on literary translation for this course as it tends to be more challenging and brings to the fore issues that could be useful when undertaking any kind of translation".

Zoe Adams Green, who is based in Rome, said,

To be honest, job offers (volume and price) have been affected very little by the pandemic. This may partly be due to the fact that I have clients (mainly agencies) all around the EU, so when there's been a full lockdown in one place, other places have been at least partially open. I may also have benefited from the typical demographic of the translation community – mainly young (ish) women with young children. As it happens, I have a toddler myself. But my husband was furloughed on full pay during full lockdown, so when the kindergarten closed, I could just go on working whilst he took care of our son. I would imagine that many translators were primary carers to their children whilst schools were closed, so the pot of translators to choose from – those still working – may have reduced, resulting in more job offers for me than I might otherwise have received. During the subsequent partial lockdown, the number of jobs I was able to take reduced because in that case, my husband had to go back to work, but the kindergarten was still closed. So I was juggling a toddler with translation jobs. Brexit hasn't affected me at all and should have a minimal impact, since I only have one client in the UK. Rendering digital services to other EU member states from Italy shouldn't be a problem. I have had a few translation jobs specifically relating to changes due to Brexit, e.g. upcoming customs changes at the end of transition.

Commenting on the situation in Germany during the pandemic, Paul Boothroyd conceded that in his business, the workflow had slowed. The fact that no trade shows and exhibitions were being held meant that no press kits were needed. The probable impact was 10–20% but, he pointed out, "at this stage in our careers that is not significant. We switched to a 4-day week in April 2019. Good move!"

Steph Kantorski, a French-to-US English translator based in San Francisco, California, mostly specialises in marketing materials for luxury/consumer goods (i.e. BIC stationery/razors, Michelin tyres, Chanel fragrances, etc.). She also does transcreation, which she loves, copywriting and auditing/consulting (Asterix & Obelix, a new TV spinoff series called "*Dogmatix and the Indomitables*"). For the first five or six months of the pandemic, from March 2020 on, Steph had almost no work for the first time in her over-20-year career, but by the last couple of months or so of 2020 things had started to pick up.

One phenomenon that Steph has seen in the last ten years or so is that of French clients correcting her English. She believes that,

> Because they learned rather poor English at school, they are unable to recognize real English. Therefore, they assume I've made a mistake (instead of the very real possibility that they don't understand what I mean). Part of that is ego, I believe, but a lot of it is a general lack of comprehension among non-linguists. Just because you speak (or have studied) a language doesn't mean you know the mechanics, idioms, local phrases, etc. This is exacerbated by the fact that the vast majority of the French learned UK English and I'm giving them real US English (which, I know, can sometimes even sound incorrect to UK speakers).

The practicalities from an interpreter's perspective

Remote interpreting and the pandemic

To gain insight into the interpreter's perspective, we interviewed four UK-based interpreters working in different language pairs/sectors and a voice coach, following up their comments with research of our own. Of all the changes that Manchester-based Kirsty Heimerl-Moggan MA has seen in a 25-year career in conference, business, and commercial legal interpreting, the greatest so far was the pandemic. Surprisingly, when we spoke in October 2020, she said her business had benefited from the disruption in working practices because "It doesn't matter anymore where I am based. I have good internet connections, and a well-equipped office with two computers and large mikes that meet the latest specs". Before this, conference-level interpreters based, for example, in the north of England like Kirsty were sometimes disadvantaged because prospective clients were inclined to prioritise those who were London-based. The misconception was that being in or near the capital meant that the interpreter was more likely to be on time for meetings anywhere in the world, yet Kirsty could get to the local airport by taxi in a matter of minutes. Now her location is immaterial – the important thing is being a good interpreter. To achieve this high level in her profession, Kirsty first studied at the Sprachen- und Dolmetscherinstitut interpreting school in Munich and then completed an MA in Conference Interpreting at the University of Salford.

Amelia Naranjo-Romero MA DPSI RPSI MCIL MAPCI MAIT, an English–Spanish interpreter said,

> During this Covid-19 pandemic remote interpreting has been very useful indeed, so I think it is here to stay at least for several years. I've been "attending" meetings and several CPD webinars via Zoom. Also, Microsoft has allowed me to do several interpreting assignments. I must say that I am enjoying working from home.

She added, "Remote interpreting has its pro and cons. It all depends on the various scenarios that interpreters encounter". "Face-to-face (FTF) interpreting is very important in healthcare, immigration, police stations and courts", she said. These involve consecutive, short simultaneous, whispering modes or sight translation, which may not be viable remotely, and body language is also very important.

Zoé Brill Diderich, a London-based lecturer in interpreting and a freelance interpreter, has colleagues working in courts who were given headsets with a mike because they could not whisper simultaneously into the client's ear anymore because of COVID-19, which made it more like a conference interpreting set-up. She too stressed the importance to interpreters of visual clues.

Frances Parkes, a voice coach who works with interpreters and actors and other professionals and who has taught voice skills on the MA Interpreting course at London Metropolitan University, told us that an online option in arbitration agreements, when interpreters are required to work on the case, is to get the interpreter to sign an NDA and submit their interpretation in note form.

Zoé specialises in and teaches/assesses health and legal interpreting between English–French/French–English at public-service level and is a tutor for conference interpreting from English into French. She thought that remote interpreting over the telephone was likely to be far more challenging for mental health appointments because "You're not communicating at the same level, so the service user may not be able to open up in the same way, and there is far less privacy". There was also the worry that confidentiality would not be taken into account. The client might be overheard by family members or other persons present in the background and likewise the interpreter might be overheard by other people where they live. Moreover, in face-to-face settings, interpreters can have a minute with clients to explain their role, but online you just go straight into the conversation, and no such introductions are made.

Amelia also mentioned unexpected problems, such as failing connections and software glitches. "A poor Wi-Fi connection can ruin a session and there is not always instant technical support at hand". She works only with private clients and although her workflow decreased slightly with the pandemic, some of her clients have been using her skills for interpreting assignments online and for translation services. The most important thing for her is that they are willing to pay reasonable fees.

The advantage of remote interpreting is not having to travel. The disadvantage is that there can be a lot of sound interference if you do not have the luxury of a quiet place where you can interpret, Zoé told us. "You need to have reliable technology and learn how to get to grips with virtual interpreting booths. Conference interpreters are sharing online their experiences of which headsets work best, and of using double screens for remote interpreting", she added, stressing the need to be very flexible and open to using different technologies. "Those who cannot do this will be left trailing behind", she warned.

Zoé agreed that remote interpreting is here to stay, but that it will be used in a different capacity, such as just telephone interpreting where the call is connected via an agency. "The NHS would not want to use Zoom as it is considered to be an unsafe platform by them (even though they have introduced the waiting room system). I don't feel they will all be comfortable with using Microsoft Teams. It also requires a patient to have this software. If both the client and service provider are in the same room, then the interpreter might as well be there too", she pointed out. She also told us that Zoom interpreting for conferences is effective, with other platforms such as Televic & Sanako being used at high-level meetings but added that the UN has said that it costs them more to run their interpreting online.

Kirsty said flexibility was very important so that you can adapt to the market. Amelia added, "In these challenging times, interpreters have to be prepared to accommodate and adapt; IT skills and knowledge have to be improved".

Although Kirsty did some general court and police work in the past, her main specialisms now are conferences and commercial legal cases that involve high-level simultaneous interpreting and require a knowledge of medical, legal and technical terminology. Not only do you have to be able to switch between modes and industrial sectors, but you also need to have excellent people skills, so that you feel comfortable talking to workers on the shop floor in a paper mill one minute, for instance, and the next find yourself interacting with your interpreting client, the CEO of a large insurance company.

A new business trend highlighted by Kirsty was more frequent small meetings and briefings due to the surge in videoconferencing and remote interpreting that was brought on by the pandemic. The overheads are very much lower than for face-to-face (FTF) and there are no travel, accommodation or subsistence costs. Clients can therefore afford to have extra meetings.

Zoé painted a very different picture in the community interpreting sector where she thought the pandemic had further exacerbated a bad situation, eradicating face-to-face bookings for herself and others. With all the community work being done over the telephone in the services she worked for, she wondered whether face-to-face would ever be reinstated. Many community interpreters she trained had been calling her in desperation to ask if she knew of anywhere they could work face-to-face since they were not able to survive on calls where they were paid around 30p/minute with no minimum hourly rate! Interpreters working at a community level are often refugees and may not always have the highest income, and don't necessarily have PCs or laptops. Even so they are very valuable, yet they are not sufficiently valued.

The status of the interpreting profession

This lecturer in interpreting has seen some worrying changes in how interpreters are treated, particularly at the community level, where a large proportion of women are employed. She outlined some of the difficulties interpreters face, such as having to work out their own technological issues, invest in new kit and have far fewer bookings.

> Overall, the industry is letting down interpreters, who are not properly protected. They have seen their hourly rates decrease consistently over the last 20

years. There is even less job security than before, since in-house (NHS) interpreting services are almost extinct (certainly in London, where we have about three units left).

At the time of writing, Barts Health NHS Trust still had an in-house interpreting service, covering languages as diverse as Bengali/Sylheti, Cantonese, Vietnamese, Turkish, Somali, Polish, Hindi/Urdu, Gujarati, Russian, Romanian and French (www.bartshealth.nhs.uk/interpreting-services, last accessed on 27.10.20). Within the health sector, budget and service cuts have meant that patients may now be asked to bring along their own interpreter to GP appointments and the interpreter may be a friend or family member. Sofia Sarfraz, a senior clinical fellow in paediatrics and medical education writing in *The BMJ* journal, concedes that this solution may be necessary in an emergency, but advises medical colleagues to use someone who is impartial.

For patients who don't share your language the gold standard is to use a professional interpreter. We've all, however, used patients' family members or other health professionals as interpreters in consultations. It's hard to see how medicine could function in our multicultural society without them, especially in emergencies. But non-professional interpreters should be used with caution and you should consider the risks. Medical interpreters have training and experience, which family members and other health professionals may lack. Interpreters should be neutral and passive, which may prove difficult for family. A family member may also give you their own version of events, and their emphasis may skew the whole consultation. It can also be difficult to check the veracity of the interpretation. This could lead to a misdiagnosis.

Similarly, a family member may find it hard to share difficult or bad news and they may have emotional or cultural reasons to distort your message. Or they may simply be bashful. Be aware that over-reliance on minors as translators can cause them harm. This can range from the child being taken out of school to act as an interpreter, to being traumatised by their exposure to a complex medical communication scenario.

(*www.bmj.com/content/368/bmj.m447, last accessed on 27.10.20*)

Court interpreting in the UK

Since the MOJ contract was privatised in 2011, many court interpreters who used to obtain work through the National Register of Public Service Interpreters now have to work through an agency and have suffered reduced rates. "From then on the interpreting profession has been in constant decline", Amelia said. The problems inherent in the three-tiered qualifications-based salary system used in the courts were discussed in Parliament back in 2013 but we were not able to find information that suggested there had been any substantial improvements since then. On 9 March 2012, Catherine Lillington reported in the *Birmingham Mail* how, to highlight the problem of inadequate checking by a Ministry of Justice-backed agency, one interpreter registered her pet rabbit Jajo with the agency, and he received an email offering him work in court! (www.birminghammail.co.uk/news/ local-news/jajo-the-rabbit-hired-as-translator-at-birmingham-180747).

Assignments are classified by agencies as complex and non-complex bookings. In the courts, checks are conducted on the quality of interpreting, but agencies may sometimes employ people without checking their qualifications and applicants desperate for work may not always tell the truth.

Amelia said,

> Interpreting is a skilled profession that requires training, education and experience.... Qualified and experienced interpreters are unable to survive in the interpreting profession with the current rates and poor terms and conditions (T&Cs). Many have been seeking another source of income and even a career change. This is a huge waste of professional skills.
>
> Agencies have been recruiting bilingual people, especially university students. The newcomers have been accepting very low rates and poor T&Cs. Then when these students graduate and move on, they will not consider interpreting as a career path because of the rates and T&Cs. Unfortunately, the damage is being done.
>
> All the above have brought unintended consequences: the decimation of the pool of public service interpreters, which has caused a detrimental impact on the public service interpreting profession and it has seriously compromised British justice."

She pointed out the detrimental effect that such trends have on job satisfaction: "A fair monetary compensation is very important, which means being able to remain working as an interpreter and being able to put aside some money for a rainy day. All this is what job satisfaction is about".

Mike Orlov, the Executive Director of the National Register of Public Service Interpreters, helped us to understand the different levels of qualifications within the profession. These can range from a Level 3 or 4 Certificate in Community Interpreting, to a CIoL Diploma in Public Service Interpreting (DPSI), which is Level 6 or graduate level, or even to an MA degree in Conference Interpreting (Level 7). To be on the National Register, you need 400 hours' experience as well as a Level 6 qualification. He explained that it was austerity in the UK public sector in 2011–2012 that had led to the outsourcing of court interpreting. This seemed to be ironic since it was the judiciary that had first perceived the need for a National Register and had provided the impetus for it to be established. The police was the second organisation to do so yet now it is far more aware of the importance of using professionally registered interpreters, he added.

In the autumn of 2020, Kirsty was still working FTF in a commercial case in one of the handful of courts that were still set up for socially distanced use, and she noted that a reverse scenario was happening. Rather than flying a German witness to the north-west of England to give evidence at considerable cost, the court placed the interpreter in the witness box – socially distanced of course. The consecutive interpreting was done with the witness remaining in Germany but appearing on screen through a video link.

A simultaneous Mandarin conference interpreter we spoke to, who works in the business sector, explained that, since the pandemic, Chinese delegates had not been able to visit the UK, so her workload had been reduced considerably. She felt that some clients might be reluctant to have online meetings. However, she was still receiving some online work and remained optimistic about the future, where she anticipates there will be a combination of online and offline work. She said that all her work was now RSI (remote simultaneous interpreting) and there appeared to be virtually no online consecutive interpreting work available – over most of 2020 it was all simultaneous, with interpreters working in pairs and alternating around every 20 minutes. All the work she had done was mainly medical-related for the private sector, for pharmaceutical companies, for example.

In addition to feeling a bit more isolated, there were also technical problems associated with working from home because you couldn't hear your partner's interpretation and so you couldn't tell when they had finished their sentence, which she found rather disconcerting. She had also had to invest in a new laptop, extra headsets and a better microphone and a more reliable internet connection. In a booth the sound quality was better, and it was easier to concentrate, since there were fewer distractions than at home.

It depends mainly on the client as to which platform is used. The Zoom platform worked well for the Chinese–English language combination, but she thought there were no options for relay interpreting though some other platforms did allow this. Further searches on https://devforum.zoom.us revealed that some interpreters have managed to work around this problem by using a second device. Relay interpreting means translating a speech into a third language or pivot language common to a large number of interpreters, who then interpret the speech into other less widely spoken languages. Few interpreters are able to offer a language pair such as Greek–Hungarian, for instance, so they work through a relay language such as English or French.

A new problem is the loneliness of the long-distance interpreter. Kirsty loves her job but said that some of her colleagues were feeling a bit isolated and everyone was missing being able to slip out of the booth for a quick chat by the coffee machine. Now they had to send each other photos of their cup of coffee via What's App in order to stay connected! These were colleagues who already knew each other in person but it might be harder to forge new friendships in the absence of any face-to-face interaction.

The future of the profession

Kirsty sees the future as being a hybrid. Both interpreters and clients have been missing FTF interaction but the ability to arrange more meetings without a prohibitive financial outlay means that remote facilities will continue to be used. For the new generation of interpreters, such as the students she trains (bilaterally) at the University of Central Lancashire, most of whom are native speakers of German, the cognitive load is much higher – they have to juggle with platforms, consoles and software from the very start.

Amelia said,

> Many people in the interpreting world would say that its future is uncertain, but from my perspective as a qualified and registered interpreter (bound to a professional code) and as a former Secretary of the National Union of Professional Interpreters and Translators (NUPIT) for twelve years, I would say it is bleak.

She reiterated the undervaluing of the interpreter's profession and added,

> Some of the technological advances available now have proven to be very detrimental to human interpreters. No doubt that some are positives, but others are being used to do the job more "efficiently," just to save time and money … Also, interpreters can be located anywhere in the world, offering cheaper rates.

Zoé, meanwhile, has noticed that at least in London there are more English native speakers training to be French interpreters than before. She does not think that automatic or machine interpreting technology has proven to be better than humans just yet but feels that interpreting is a difficult job to manage, unless you can work as both a conference interpreter and public service interpreter, and/or add translation to your skill set. Working as a community interpreter for public services in the UK, especially when telephone interpreting only, simply does not offer a realistic salary to live on at the moment, she concluded. Luckily NUPIT (National Union of Professional Interpreters and Translators and a branch of the trade union Unite) has been very active in trying to improve the situation, as have the ITI (Institute of Translation and Interpreting) and the CIoL (Chartered Institute of Linguists).

Frances believes that in the future,

> The best interpreters will work. Professionals, such as specialist doctors who give talks to fellow professionals about their work and research, need interpreters whom they can trust and rely on. I think it will be a lot to do with the communication skills of the interpreter, their presentation, and their ability, while they are interpreting, to reflect the values of the person they are interpreting for. Conference interpreters will always be in demand.

A key asset for interpreters, Kirsty pointed out, is the ability to be diplomatic in such a way that the client appreciates the fact that you have taken the onus off them. If you need to chase up an agenda for a meeting, rather than saying "I haven't been sent the agenda", you can apply your emotional intelligence and make it sound as if you think there might be a possible problem with emails having arrived or suchlike! Or if they are not quite clear how to proceed with their interpreted meeting, you can sell a suggestion to them by saying something along the lines of "I'm not quite sure how you were planning to do this but another client of mine usually does it like this ... Would that be all right with you?" The need to be a good communicator was also cited by Frances, the voice coach.

Resources for interpreters

When it comes to resources, Kirsty relies predominantly on parallel reading of specialist material, such as websites intended for doctors (for medical interpreting assignments). She keeps her glossaries in Excel files with five or six columns, which allows her to note all the relevant source and client information. She always does lots of preparation, which helps her to remain a much sought-after professional.

Zoé uses Siri to convert her notes into text when needed to keep a record of ideas but doesn't use any other software systems. For her research she uses word reference.com and proz.com plus a range of different dictionaries and thesauri.

There are various other software tools available to interpreters, such as speech recognition, Otter.ai (for artificial intelligence-based speech to text transcription), Interpreters' Help for high-speed glossary look-up both online and offline, and Nebo (an application that is used to convert handwritten notes on an i-Pad into text). Techforword (which runs online courses for language professionals) provides a number of free resources on its website (www.techforword.com) and YouTube channel.

A useful resource for interpreting researchers working with German and recommended on the ITI German network e-group is DGD: Datenbank für Gesprochenes Deutsch (dgd.ids-mannheim.de). This site has a home page available in both English and German, listing a number of useful publications. Registered users can access 34 different corpora covering various dialects, the German spoken in areas such as Australia, Israel, Namibia, Russia and the Americas, and on German reunification and present-day German.

It remains to be seen how British interpreters working in the EU will fare in the next few years. Will more work go to those of other nationalities but with English as their L1 (to Irish interpreters, for instance)?

Sources of market information in the professional language sector

Developments in technology are both complex and continue to evolve from month to month but we have attempted to signpost publications that highlight some of the trends at the time of writing. Useful sources of information relevant to ongoing developments in both interpreting and translation include the *ITI Bulletin*, *The Linguist* and https://techforword.com. Some features from the very informative *ATA Chronicle* published by the American Translators' Association are available online at https://www.atanet.org/chronicle/ and updates of technological developments and news from all aspects of the language industry are provided by Slator (https://slator. com), an organisation co-founded by a master's graduate in Translation from the University of Westminster.

An agency's viewpoint

In autumn 2020, we spoke to Clare Suttie of Atlas Translations in St Albans, which went on to win the ATC Translation Company of the Year award that December. Clare told us that things had massively changed since she started the agency in 1991 with

> a PC, Wordperfect 2.0, and a modem someone found under their bed! We are a small, but perfectly formed agency, who have weathered recessions, and the Brexit referendum (that really was awful), and now a pandemic, so I can confidently say that we must be doing something right. And as a small agency, it can be hard for us to keep up with everything as far as technology goes, but we do our best.

Atlas employs a team of six, working a four-day week. Some of the project managers have a postgraduate translation qualification, too. "Those translators who have worked as project managers beforehand or who have an office background will find it easier to set themselves up as freelances because they understand how the business world works", she added.

"I have my own views on how the translators who are doing well are achieving this – by being much more proactive businesspeople", Clare continued. "As an agency, we were guilty of being in a position where work would come to us by word-of-mouth recommendation, with not too much effort. These days everyone has to work harder to be heard and to be noticed in amongst all the noise and clatter". She advised emerging translators to work on their marketing and publicity skills – using social media and platforms such as LinkedIn to their advantage. It's also helpful to find a niche, that is, an area that they can specialise in and hopefully enjoy.

It is much harder now for newly qualified translators to gain experience than it was in the 1980s and 1990s, even if they are extremely talented. One way of doing this, Clare suggests, is to do a work placement or internship or failing that, to carry out some pro bono work for an organisation such as Translators without Borders or an international charity. One of her tips is to ask these "clients" to supply you with references, which you can then use when you apply to agencies.

The demand for specific subject areas and languages fluctuates, with German into English now being at a premium since the demise of many university German departments in the UK, which has led to fewer schools offering German.

We also asked about checking and revising (and standardising in the case where jobs have to be split), especially for TM output. We wanted to know whether the in-house team did any of that or whether the agency only used translators whose work was already of a high standard and relied on them to check everything meticulously.

Clare said,

> it depends on the job! We will always quote for these stages – so for every translation we will offer translation, proofreading against the original text, and checking (at least once, and more, depending whether a third party has added errors!). For jobs that have been split, we will price to include a revision – and we will do this in-house if the language involved is covered by one of the team.

She agreed that, with editing and revising, it is important to know when to stop. Her agency is rigorous in the screening of applications from freelances.

> All the translators we use are suitably qualified, and we do make people who want to work with us fill in a long form and provide referees, whom we do actually contact! We reject more people than we accept, often because people don't complete the form properly or have a fear of providing us with client details for references.

You can also attend their open days, open to all, and held twice a year. From mid-2020, Atlas have started asking new applicants to chat with them either online or by phone before being issued with a password to proceed to the application form. This approach allows both parties to ensure there is a good fit of experience, language, subject area – and the subject of rates can be openly discussed.

Clare added, "If you would like to apply, you will need to have at least one of the following":

1. A recognised qualification in advanced translation studies and at least two years' documented relevant experience.
2. An equivalent qualification and at least three years' documented relevant experience.
3. Five years or more of documented relevant professional experience.

You can find more detailed information on working with Atlas at www.atlas-translations.co.uk/translators-faq/.

A prime example of an enterprising young professional who adopted the proactive kind of approach that Clare referred to was featured in "The translator's kitchen diaries" on pages 8–11 of the November–December 2020 edition of the *ITI Bulletin*. Hannah Lawrence, a freelance translator from French into English decided to cook and translate one recipe a week, which she then wrote about in her blog *"That Translator Can Cook"*. This has given her the opportunity to gain knowledge, and clients, in the culinary field.

PAUSE FOR THOUGHT 2

Can you identify any limitations of MT or "robot translators"?

Do you think "robot writers" are more likely to become widely established than robot translators? Why do you believe this is or is not the case?

Passion, professionalism and the quest for perfection: are they enough?

All the colleagues we spoke to were keen to stress the importance and benefits of human language professionals, whose expertise needs to be seen by the public as having equal status to that of accountants, for instance. For Tim Morgan, passion and professionalism clearly are enough. His annual output is around one million words! However, he has developed a wide range of specialisms in aspects of law, medicine, pharmaceuticals and naval matters (marine accidents, marine engineering, litigation, navigation and mariners' materials). He can draft up to 2500 words an hour, so typing is not a problem and work dictated using speech recognition software takes him longer to edit. "When text is very repetitive, searching in MS Word and then copying and pasting is perfectly swift", he said.

One conclusion that emerged from our interviews was that there remains a need for language professionals of high calibre who can produce premium work, such as very carefully translated documents for law firms engaged in court cases or back-translations of clinical study documents for pharmaceutical companies. Tim Morgan pointed out that in the latter example, translators were not permitted to use translation software. He added:

> The real reason why human translators will always be necessary is that almost no-one says precisely and fully what they mean. The gap between the surface meaning and the actual proposition is always there, and AI can't bridge that. Most people, most of the time, speak and write sloppily. Poorly chosen words; badly constructed sentences; logical ellipses, etc. Humans are needed to bridge the gap.
>
> *(Personal communication, 19.11.20)*

As we explained in Chapter 4, careful planning of CPD could help you to achieve professional success. The information on market trends and the individual career trajectories highlighted in the present chapter are intended to further equip you with the insights you will need to identify your own current and potential skill set. Technological advances mean that the ability to provide premium work is what will allow the language professionals of the future to acquire a competitive edge.

PAUSE FOR THOUGHT 3: SUMMARY WRITING

Imagine that you are writing an article for a blog or website aimed at students of translation and/or interpreting. Take another look at the section on summary writing in Chapter 4, then try to summarise the main findings that emerged from our interviews of language professionals. You should aim to write around 1000 words.

To help you, the main questions we asked can be found in the e-resources available for this book at www.routledge.com/9780367683252.

CONCLUSION

In the previous five chapters we have considered various aspects of social and cultural change from two main perspectives: its effects on the evolution of language itself, and its repercussions on the language professions. We have highlighted some practical steps that practitioners can take to embrace change and at the same time enhance and extend their skills, ensuring that they can survive and even thrive.

Translators and interpreters need to keep abreast of new linguistic developments, not only in their target language, but also in their source language. To this end, it is advisable to compile glossaries of new terminology, politically acceptable language and/or spelling conventions and update them on a regular basis. In our analysis of English texts and translation comparisons, we have explained the key factors to look for when you are presented with a source text that contains new concepts and expressions. The Guidance Table set out in Chapter 2 and the annotated translations included in Chapter 3 aim to provide further insights into how to deal with change and provide your clients with work of optimal quality. Further opportunities to practise and enhance your skills are offered in the e-resources.

To widen your understanding of recent changes in your source culture, you could read some of the latest novels, browse its national press and study books about current affairs or recent history, such as, for example, *Why the Germans Do it Better*, which provides an excellent analysis of how Germany is coping with contemporary challenges (Kampfner 2020). One example of the impact of social trends on the translation profession was the controversy that arose in early 2021 over who should be allowed to translate work by the young US Black poet Amanda Gorman. Amanda performed her work at the inauguration ceremony for US President Joe Biden. Soon after this, foreign publishers began commissioning translators to produce versions of "The Hill we Climb" in various languages but, before long, both a Dutch and a Catalan translator had ceased work on the project. The debate was reported by Dorany Pineda in the Los Angeles Times on 22 March

DOI: 10.4324/9781003136903-7

2021 (www.latimes.com) in a feature entitled "Amanda Gorman translation back-lash sparks racial controversy". The issue was whether the identity of the translator should match that of the poet. The American Literary Translators Association responded with a statement in which it said,

> ALTA acknowledges that racial equity remains unrealized in the literary translation community, both in and outside of the United States.
>
> The question of whether identity should be the deciding factor in who is allowed to translate whom is a false framing of the issues at play. ALTA believes that if translators felt authorized to translate only those with whom they share an identity, it would be damaging to literary translation as a practice and as a profession. But in fact, translators choose or are chosen to translate works based on a complex network of factors including affinity, perceived status or skill, the author's own wishes, the desires of publishers, and so on. Legitimising translation according to a simplistic schema of identity matching would be a problem, but that is not what occurred in this case. In our view, the foundational problem this controversy reveals is the scarcity of Black translators and other translators of colour, a scarcity caused by long-term patterns of discrimination in education and publishing.
>
> *(https://mailchi.mp/literarytranslators/alta-statement-on-racial-equality-in-translation)*

In order to demonstrate its commitment to diversity, back in 2016 the ALTA set up the annual Peter K. Jansen Memorial Travel Fellowship, which is preferentially awarded to an emerging translator of colour or a translator working from an underrepresented diaspora or stateless language. In 2020, it established the ALTA BIPOC Caucus – a space for literary translators who identify as Black, Indigenous and/or as a person of colour.

As the *LA Times* article points out, the issue of identity extends far beyond that of race to areas such as age, gender and sexual orientation. The controversy appears to have spread to translation from the #OwnVoices movement, which maintains that stories about marginalised people should be written by authors who share the same identity and experiences. That debate was sparked in 2015 by Jeanine Cummins' bestseller *American Dirt*, a thriller about Mexican refugees written by a white American. Pineda says that translation "is inherently about making work accessible to audiences different from the author". She quotes an email from the Congolese writer Alain Mabanckou, who says that two of the main influences on his writing were Toni Morrison and Maya Angelou, whom he was able to read in his native French thanks to female white translators.

But what are the future prospects for our industry in general? According to the findings of the ITI Autumn 2020 Pulse Survey (www.iti.org.uk/resource/pulse-survey-a-challenging-marketplace-but-increased-positivity.html), 39% of respondents were still feeling positive about the future of the translation and interpreting sector and 58% had gained new business over the last 12 months although 54% said work from existing clients had decreased. Most members (61%) had managed to maintain their rates at a similar level, with 25% seeing a reduction and 13% an improvement, whilst 50% of respondents said the impact of COVID-19 on their business lives had remained much the same since the April survey.

A key theme highlighted by respondents to the Pulse Survey in autumn 2020 was the need to adapt to fit their working lives round family commitments (particularly while schools were closed) and to diversify. Some clients had even asked language professionals to reduce their rates – with interpreters being particularly severely affected by this and by the lower volume of work coming through. Yet the pandemic also resulted in new types of work for some 30% of all respondents, including healthcare-related procedures; organisational procedures and policies, including health and safety documents; communications about how organisations had been dealing with and performing in relation to the situation; and promotional activities for products and services. In the spring 2021 Pulse Survey of ITI members, the questions showed a strong focus on CPD, which professional linguists now find increasingly important.

As some colleagues mentioned in the interviews we conducted for Chapters 4 and 5, and in "Distanced voices", a feature that appeared in the July–August 2020 issue of *ITI Bulletin* (pp. 16–17), interpreters had to adapt in 2020 in order to work remotely, and many had to invest in more sophisticated technology. Many translators have been undergoing more CPD than ever before, seizing the opportunity to acquire further transferable skills whenever there is a lull in their working schedule. Professional organisations such the ITI, CIoL and ATA and universities, such as London Metropolitan University and UCL, responded to the pandemic situation by offering a wide range of short online courses, seminars and workshops on topics that include: various aspects of business and career development, specialist areas such as consecutive note-taking, copywriting, legal translation, localisation, machine translation post-editing, marketing texts, providing certified translations, re-speaking, scientific writing, subtitling, the beauty business and translation tools. Training opportunities within language networks covered pandemic-related terminology, inclusive language and patent terminology.

Many linguists working from or with the UK have had to get to grips with the implications of Brexit and new regulations for their business. Excellent advice on such matters is available to members of e-groups within the various professional associations and to the translation and interpreting community on Twitter and LinkedIn, but you generally need to join up or register first to access the wealth of information that colleagues are willing to share. The extra expense that investments in membership subscriptions, courses, hardware and software entail can be offset against tax but there is no doubt that some practitioners are worried to see that machine translation tools are becoming even more widely used and fear for the future. Even institutions such as the US Citizenship and Immigration Services are said to be using Google Translate, according to the non-profit organisation ProPublica (*ITI Bulletin*, November–December 2019). This is worrying news when it is a case of machine translation being used to decide whether refugees should be allowed into the US. Earlier that year, however, professionals derived some comfort from an article in the March–April issue, where the translation technology developer Lilt told the *Bulletin*'s technology columnist Jost Zetzsche that "Translation is an art form and Lilt's focus is on how we can continue to develop technology that uses AI (artificial intelligence) to enable translators to do their best work". The notion that translation memory and machine translation and machine interpreting systems are seen as an adjunct to, rather than a replacement for, human translation and interpreting is reassuring. Long may this continue.

But what of the more distant future of language in generations to come? In "How will language change if humans travel the stars?", Sam Kean postulates that the language spoken by astronauts on a mission to Mars could mutate so much that nobody would understand their descendants if they were able to return to Earth a couple of centuries later (https://slate.com/technology/2020/08/interstellar-tra vel-language-change-linguistic-evolution.html, accessed on 31.8.2020). As we have explained in this book, "language changes when *people* find themselves in new social situations, because they need new ways of describing their reality," Sam says.

> Living your entire life inside a rocket ship certainly qualifies as novel. Language also mutates quickly when a small group of speakers is isolated for an extended time—and no one in human history would be more isolated than the colonists.

Two US linguistics experts, Andrew McKenzie, and Jeffrey Punske have considered the possible effects of space travel on language, trying to determine factors that could trigger language change during interstellar exploration, compared with previous exploratory voyages and the colonisation of New Zealand and Texas, for example (www.people.ku.edu/~a326m085/2019-ESA-Interstellar-BG.pdf). The landing of the robot helicopter 'Perseverance' on Mars in spring 2021 clearly heralds exciting times with potential opportunities for the professional linguists of the future, when effective communication could be more crucial than ever.

GLOSSARY

Note: The asterisked definitions below are directly cited from the following publications: *Thinking Italian Translation* Second Edition (Cragie et al. 2016: 189–196); *Thinking English Translation* (Cragie & Pattison 2018: 118–124); *Translation: A Guide to the Practice of Crafting Target Texts* (Cragie & Pattison 2020: 140–146).

abstracting	writing a summary of a scientific text.
ambiguity*	a situation in which either the **ST** or the **TT** can be interpreted in two different ways.
archaic*	(language) lexis or style evoking earlier or historical language or created to produce a period effect.
binary gender	classification of gender in two opposite forms (masculine and feminine).
binomial	a two-part name derived from Latin.
Brexit	the process by which the UK withdrew from the European Union.
calque	a word or phrase borrowed from another language and translated literally.
CAT tool	a computer-assisted translation tool.
clarity*	the ability to express a message in simple and unambiguous terms.
code-switching	moving from one social context or linguistic register to another.
coherence*	the underlying structural links between the ideas within a text. In combination with cohesion, it determines the cogency of an argument.

DOI: 10.4324/9781003136903-8

cohesion*	the surface-based structural links between the words within a text that make it flow smoothly by means of lexical or grammatical devices.
coin/coinage	inventing a new word or phrase.
collocations*	the use of words (a noun and an adjective, a noun and a verb, a verb and an adverb) in combination. Where a non-standard collocation is used, this will attract the reader's attention.
colonialism	domination of one country or people by another more powerful one.
compound	a lexical unit consisting or two or more components, usually nouns.
connotation*	an overtone, implication or associated meaning embodied by a word.
conservative prescriptivism (or linguistic prescription)	rules governing perceived correctness of language.
context* (adj. **contextual)**	the cultural background to a text and/or the professional framework to the translation task.
contextualisation*	provision of a meaningful context to a text.
copywriting	writing advertising or marketing texts.
creative writing	texts produced following a craft-like approach, as opposed to writing for academic, technical, specialist and (non-literary) professional purposes.
cultural diffusion	spreading of beliefs, values and other sociocultural phenomena from one social group to another.
culture*	the artistic, historical, political and sociological background in the area or areas where a language is spoken.
Denglish	"a variety of German containing a high proportion of English words" (www.dictionary.com/browse/denglish; last accessed on 07.05.21).
dialect*	a regional language variety with non-standard features.
discourse*	the ordered and coherent expression of ideas in text or speech.
domestication*	a term coined by Lawrence Venuti (1995: 20) for the process in which the translator brings the TT into line with the TC, making the text seem far less foreign.
edit*	to make a final check before publication of the **TT**, focusing on the style and presentation and ensuring that no typing errors have crept in.
elegant variation	a way of avoiding repetition by using alternative expressions.

encoding	the process of expressing in the target language the message contained in the source text.
Estuary (English)	a variety of modified regional speech that originated by the banks of the Thames and its estuary. The term appears to have been first used by UK linguist David Rosewarne on 19 October 1984 in an article for the Times Educational Supplement.
ethnographica	the collective artefacts typical of a race or people.
etymon	a word from a foreign language giving rise to a loan-word.
expansion *	explanation of the **SL** item in the **TL**.
extra-contextual (references) *	the mentioning of items that are extrinsic to the subject matter and immediate context of the **ST**.
formality *	a scale that measures the level of sophistication of the language used in a given social setting.
format (or **form**) *	the physical layout and non-lexical features of a text.
fronting *	an action that brings forward information from elsewhere in a sentence.
gender-neutral language (GNL)	language that does not distinguish between masculine and feminine forms.
generalisation *	the use of a general as against a specific term.
genre * (or **text-type**)	a category to which, in a given culture, a given text is seen to belong and within which it is seen to share a type of communicative purpose with other texts; that is, the text is seen to be more or less typical of the genre.
gloss *	a brief explanation, usually inserted in brackets into the text, of a word or phrase deemed unlikely to be known or understood by the target readership.
glottal stop	"a consonant formed by the audible release of the airstream after complete closure of the glottis" (https://languages.oup.com/google-dictionary-en; last accessed on 08.09.20). It is commonly used in South London accents.
graphic novel	text combining words and images.
herd immunity	"When most of a population is immune to an infectious disease, *herd immunity* provides indirect protection (also called *herd protection*) to those who are not immune to the disease" (as defined by Johns Hopkins University).
hypercorrection	use of an incorrect form of lexis or pronunciation caused by a misplaced analogy with another form.
IATE	Interactive Terminology for Europe (shared terminological database of the European Union).

idiolect*	an author's own particular style of writing, choice of words, use of figurative language, and tone, sometimes referred to as the author's voice.
inclusivity	providing equal access to all participants regardless of gender, class, race, etc.
inference*	a meaning that is suggested or implied 'between the lines' in a text, leading the reader to make assumptions.
informality	natural and spontaneous expression of language.
language variation	an intermediate or transitional stage before final acceptance in the host language.
learning outcomes*	the skills that students or readers are expected to acquire as a result of attending a course or completing a module.
lexicon	a vocabulary or language.
lexis (adj. **lexical**)*	vocabulary, terminology, or set of words used in a text.
linguistic prescription	(*see* conservative prescriptivism).
linguistic purism	defining or recognising one form of language as superior to another.
linguistic variable	a language, dialect, style, register, syntactic pattern or particular sound (defined by Stockwell 2007).
liquid learning	a form of education using diverse sources and channels.
literal meaning*	the primary meaning of a word.
literal translation*	a word-for-word translation that adheres closely to the **ST** but may sound unnatural and lead to **translationese**.
loan-word	a word 'borrowed' from another language.
localisation*	producing a target text in which the cultural content is adapted somewhat to match the target culture.
machine translation (MT)	an automated process by which text is translated from one language to another.
MTPE (machine translation post-editing)	human editing of machine-generated translation.
macro strategy*	the decisions the translator makes regarding how to approach the particular translation task.
meaning*	the set of messages conveyed through discourse, whether spoken or written, both at the level of its individual constituent units and in the text in its entirety.
metaphor	a figure of speech referring to one concept or object by means of another.

micro strategies *	localised decisions relating to the translation of a word, phrase or other individual unit.
model text *	a TL text with a similar subject matter or in the same genre as the ST, even if the convergence is only partial.
neologism	a newly coined or invented word.
new normal	changes that have taken place in our homes, social and work life, especially as a result of the coronavirus pandemic.
nominalisation (or **nouning**)	using a word which is not a noun as a noun.
paraphrase *	rewording the **SL** item in the **TL** to make the meaning more apparent.
permissive society	"the type of society that has existed in most of Europe, Australia and North America since the 1960s, in which there is a great amount of freedom of behaviour, especially sexual freedom" (Cambridge Dictionary online).
phrasal verb *	a verb combined with a preposition to create a new meaning of its own, such as 'bring up' or 'check in'. Very common in colloquial and informal English.
politeness *	a scale that measures where the tone or tenor of the text fits on a scale that ranges from the exceedingly polite to the very familiar.
political correctness	avoiding behaviour and actions that may exclude or offend certain social groups.
polysemy (adj. **polysemous**) *	a situation where a word has a number of possible meanings.
post-editing	see **MTPE: machine translation post-editing**.
pro bono(work)	work undertaken free of charge or at a lower cost.
purpose (of a text) *	to inform, stimulate debate, criticise/praise, recommend, offer an opinion, etc. It may not always be obvious, as in the case of satire, for example.
received pronunciation (RP)	an accent recognised as 'British' typically without a specific regional form.
reduction *	simplification and shortening of the **SL** item in the **TL**.
register *	level of language used for a particular purpose or used in a specific setting.
remote interpreting	interpretation between parties in different locations using various means of communication.
repurposed (of language)	lexis that has acquired a new connotation or meaning from the original one or ones.

restructuring*	an action in which the 'shape' of the sentence is changed, in terms of syntax and word-order, to align the **TT** with **TL** discourse conventions.
revision*	checking a **TT** (often one produced using CAT tools) against the **ST** for errors, omissions and any inconsistency.
scanning	reading a text through quickly in order to extract the content and meaning.
sense translation*	a technique used to explain the meaning as clearly as possible where a reference, pun or image is not directly translatable.
sentence*	"a sequence of words capable of standing alone to make an assertion, ask a question or give a command, usually consisting of a subject and a predicate" (Collins English Dictionary and Thesaurus 21st Century Edition).
SL	see **source language**.
social register*	the language relating to a specific social setting (level of formality).
social responsibility	obligation of an individual or organisation to act in the best interests of society.
social variable	a factor "that determines a variation in language such as gender, geography, age, occupation" (Stockwell 2007).
sociolect*	a social variant of language that is used within a specific social setting.
source language*	the language in which the **ST** is expressed.
source text* (or **ST**)	the **text** requiring translation.
ST	see **source text**.
strategy*	the approach adopted by the translator, such as deciding whether to opt for a communicative or semantic translation or a combination of the two.
synonym*	a word or phrase with a similar meaning.
synonymy*	a situation where words are identical or nearly identical in meaning.
syntax*	the structure of words into phrases or sentences.
target culture*	the cultural, geographical and social setting in which the **TT** will be used.
target language* (or **TL**)	the language into which the **ST** is to be translated.
target readership*	the readers at whom the target text is aimed.
target text* (or **TT**)	the **text** that is a translation of the **ST**.
text*	a coherent piece of writing in a given language.
text-type	see **genre**.

theme*	existing information about a topic.
TL	see **target language**.
transcreation	transposing the message to adapt it to the target culture/s rather than simply 'translating it'.
transferable skills	a range of skills or a skill set that can be applied across diverse sectors.
translation brief*	information relevant to the translation assignment and the intended function of the **TT** that is supplied by the client, work provider or exam setter.
translation memory (TM)	a database consisting of segments that matches (previously translated) source and target texts.
TT	see **target text**.
uptalk	the practice of ending a sentence on a rising note.
viewpoint*	the perspective of the text, whether it is fact or allegation, the author's own views, and so on.

BIBLIOGRAPHY

Alemani, L. Covid, finde, faláfel, vigoréxico … Las nuevas palabras del Diccionario de la Lengua en 2020. *El Mundo*, 30. 11. 20.

Anderson, E. ed. When equity release is a good idea, in the Money section of *The i Newspaper*, 9. 9. 20.

Baccolini, R. and Zanettin, F. 2008. The Language of Trauma, Art Spiegelmann's Maus and its Translations, in Zanettin, F. (ed) *Comics in Translation*, Manchester: St Jerome.

Baksh, M. Book Review: The whole picture: The colonial story of the art in our museums and why we need to talk about it, (2020) by Alice Procter. *Art Quarterly*, Autumn 2020.

Begag, A. 1986. *Le Gône du Chaâba*. Paris: Seuil (Points).

Boschwitz, U.A. *Der Reisende*. Republished in 2019. Stuttgart: Klett-Kotta Verlag.

Bourne, H. 2019. The Places I've Cried in Public, from the 2019 Usborne promotional booklet.

Bowker, L. and McBride, C. 2017. Précis-writing as a form of speed training for translation students. *The Interpreter and Translator Trainer*, 11(4).

Bywood, L. 2020. Technology and Audiovisual Translation: The Road Ahead, in *The Palgrave Handbook of Audiovisual Translation and Media Accessibility*. London: Palgrave.

Bywood, L. and Nikolić, K. 2021. Trends in subtitling and related areas in Audiovisual translation: the road ahead. *Journal of Audiovisual Translation*, 4(1), 50–70. https://doi.org/10.47476/jat.v4i1.2021.156.

Clark, R. and Ivanič, R. 1997. *The Politics of Writing*. London and New York: Routledge.

Clinton, J. Gender-inclusive words banned. *The i Newspaper*, 11. 5. 2021.

Colina, S. 2015. *Fundamentals of Translation*. Cambridge: Cambridge University Press.

Collins English Dictionary – Essential Edition, 2nd edition, 2019. Glasgow: HarperCollins.

Cragie, S. and Pattison, A. 2020. *Translation – A Guide to the Practice of Crafting Target Texts*. London and New York: Routledge.

Cragie, S. and Pattison, A. 2018. *Thinking English Translation*. London and New York: Routledge.

Cragie, S., Higgins, I., Hervey, S. and Gambarotta, P. 2016. *Thinking Italian Translation*, 2nd edition. London and New York: Routledge.

Dent, S. 2020. *Dictionary corner* in the *Radio Times*, 2–8 May 2020.

Dent, S. One man's meat …. *The i Newspaper*, 24–25 October 2020.

de Souza, T. Everyone welcome. *The National Trust Magazine*, Autumn 2020.

Durkheim, E. in the Project Gutenberg eBook: *The Elementary Forms of the Religious Life* (eBook 41360)

Fricke, L. 2018. *Töchter*. Hamburg: Rowohlt.

Glickman, J. *Harvard Business Review*, 1 November 2011.

Gosling, T. It's all ova for Czech women's suffix. *The Times*, 9 July 2021.

Gronlund, M. 2020. *Wellcome Change*, *The i Newspaper*, 13. 8. 20.

Hansen. D. 2015. *Altes Land*. Munich: Albrecht Knaus Verlag.

Hargreaves, C. Root-to-leaf eating: a tasty way to cut waste. *The i Newspaper*, 13. 8. 20.

Hergé. 1930. *Tintin in the Congo*, 2016 translation by Leslie Lonsdale-Cooper and Michael Turner. Brussels: Casterman.

Houbert, F. 2005. *Guide pratique de traduction juridique – anglais–français*. Paris: La maison du dictionnaire.

Houbert, F. 2020. Dictionnaire de terminologie juridique anglais–français. Paris: La maison du dictionnaire.

Kampfner, J. 2020. *Why the Germans Do it Better*. London: Atlantic Books.

Koch, B. 2017. *Keine Stille Nacht*, translated by John Gohorry, Nottingham, UK: Shoestring Press.

Koponen, M. et al. (eds). 2021. *Translation Revision and Post-editing: Industry Practices and Cognitive Processes*. New York and London: Routledge.

Le Guin, U.K. 2018. *Dreams Must Explain Themselves – The Selected Non-Fiction of Ursula K. Le Guin*. London: Gollancz.

Lyall, S. 1998. London Journal: Britons prick up their ears: Blair's a li'l peculiar. *New York Times*, 18. 6. 98.

McCulloch, G. 2020. *Because Internet: Understanding How Language is Changing*. London: Vintage.

Meertens, R. 2021. *Guide Anglais–français de la Traduction*. Paris: Meertens.

Milford, J. 2012. In Mugglestone, L. (ed) *The Oxford History of English*, updated edition. Oxford: Oxford University Press.

Milliot, J. Print book sales rose 8.2% in 2020. *Publisher's Weekly* 7, Jan 2021.

Nadeau, J.-B., and Barlow, J. 2013. *The Story of Spanish*. New York: St Martin's Press.

Nadeau, J.-B., and Barlow, J. 2008. *The Story of French*. London: Portico Books.

Nadeau, J.-B., and Barlow, J. 2003. *Sixty Million Frenchmen can't be Wrong*. Napier Illinois: Sourcebooks, Inc.

Pratt, H. 1967. *Ballata del Mare Salato* (*Ballad of the Salty Sea*), translated for the 2020 edition by Dean Mullaney and Simone Castaldi. Eurocomics. US. San Diego: IDW Publishing.

Roig, E. 2021. *Why we Matter*. Berlin: Aufbau Verlag.

Rosewarne, D. Estuary English. *Times Educational Supplement*, 19. 10. 1984.

Shariatmadari, D. 2019. *Don't Believe a Word*. London: Weidenfeld and Nicholson.

Sherwin, A. Youngest-ever Booker Prize winner named. *The i Newspaper*, 26. 8. 2020.

Sofer, M. 2006. *The Translator's Handbook*. 6th revised edition. Rockville, Md: Schreiber Publishing.

Steils, N. et al. Implementing the liquid curriculum: the impact of virtual world learning on higher education, deposited in CURVE April 2016.

Stockwell, P. 2007. *Sociolinguistics: A Resource Book for Students*, 2nd ed., London: Routledge English Language Resources.

Topley, W.W.C. and Wilson, G.S. *The Spread of Bacterial Infection: The Problem of Herd Immunity*. *The Journal of Hygiene* (London), May 1923.

Trask, L. and Mayblin, W. 2012. *Introducing Linguistics*. London and New York: Routledge.

Urdiales-Shaw, M. 2020. The Challenges of Translating Art Spiegelmann's Maus. In *The Palgrave Handbook of Holocaust Literature and Culture*. London: Palgrave Macmillan.

Venuti, L. 1995. *The Translator's Invisibility: A History of Translation*. London and New York: Routledge.

Wilkes, D. BBC commentators are told: Don't say cakewalk, it's racist. *Daily Mail*, 9. 9. 2020.

Wilson, S. 2020. *The Library at the End of the Universe*. London: Usborne.

Wolf, N. and Hargreaves, A. 2007. *Shanty Town Kid*. Lincoln, Nebraska: University of Nebraska Press.

Yamada, M. The impact of Google machine translation on post-editing by student translators. *The Journal of Specialised Translation*, Feb 2019.

Not attributed to a particular author

The Penguin Book of Brexit Cartoons (2018).
Antiques Trade Gazette. The normal new (26. 9. 2020).

Materials accessed online

The dates in brackets indicate when the site was last accessed.

Anderson, H. How Americanisms are killing the English language, 2017, BBC News. www.bbc.com/culture/article/20170904-how-americanisms-are-killing-the-english-language (2020).

Béraud, C. and Portier, P. 2015. Mariage pour tous – The Same Sex Marriage Controversy in France. In *The Intimate. Polity and the Catholic Church: Laws about Life, Death and the Family in So-called Catholic Countries*, ed. Karel Dobbelaere and Alfonso Pérez-Agote. University of Leuven Press. http://cesor.ehess.fr/2015/03/the-intimate-polity-and-the-catholic-church/ (2020).

Capoferro, R. Individual soldier: Corto Maltese e l'immaginario coloniale. www.academia.edu/22879147/Individual_Soldier_Corto_Maltese_e_limmaginario_coloniale (2021).

Cho, K., et al. On the properties of neural machine translation: encoder–decoder approaches. https://arxiv.org/abs/1409.1259 (2020).

Engelberg, S. et al. Internet lexicography at the Leibniz-Institute for the German Language. kln.lexicala.com/kln28/ids (2020).

Fantinuoli, C. Interpreting and technology: The upcoming technological turn. University of Mainz. 209–203-1341–1341-10–20181129.pdf. https://arxiv.org/abs/1409.1259 (2020).

Gallagher E. Interview – We meet the man behind Walter. www.thecustardtv.com/2018/04/interview-we-meet-man-behind-walter.htm (2020).

Hutt, D. Why some Czechs are up in arms ova plans to drop feminised surnames. www.euronews.com/2021/06/16/why-some-czechs-are-up-in-arms-ova-plans-to-drop-feminised-surnames (2021).

Jones, G. What's the difference between translation and transcreation?https://translatorstudio.co.uk/difference-between-translation-transcreation (2021).

Joshi, S. et al. A trusted node–free eight-user metropolitan quantum communication network (published in *Science Advances*, 2 Sep 2020). www.science.org/doi/10.1126/sciadv.aba0959 (2021).

Koponen, M. Is machine translation post-editing worth the effort? A survey of research into post-editing and effort. *The Journal of Specialised Translation Issue*, 25. www.jostrans.org/issue25/art_koponen.php (2020).

McKenzie, A. and Punske, J. Language development during interstellar travel. https://indico.esa.int/event/309/attachments/3517/4664/World_Ship_Linguistics_-_Jeffrey_Punske.pdf (2020).

Meyers, S.L. and Lorenzsonn, E. In defense of 'textspeak': a socio-linguist says emojis and LOLs are modernizing English. www.wpr.org/defense-textspeak-socio-linguist-says-em ojis-and-lols-are-modernizing-english (2020).

Morris, N. No more left and right: UK's 'seven political tribes'. *The i Newspaper*, 26. 10. 2020. https://inews.co.uk/news/politics/left-and-right-political-opinion-britain-conservatives-labour-737495 (2020).

Myatt, J. English Accents – Estuary. www.word-connection.fr, 31. 08. 2020 (2020).

Navarro, R. et al. Are Romance languages becoming more gender neutral? 11. 9. 2020. https://globalvoices.org/2020/09/11/are-romance-languages-becoming-more-gender-neutral (2021).

Newman, D. and O'Brien, J. Exploring the architecture of everyday life. 2013. https://uk.sa gepub.com/sites/default/files/upm-binaries/23953_Page_442.pdf (2020).

Ono, N. and Naoko, T. Interpreting at the Olympics: a survey of the literature and interview. https://core.ac.uk/download/pdf/234718991.pdf (2020).

Parakala, K. Ten emerging trends shaping our future. www.ghd.com/en/perspectives/ten-emerging-trends-shaping-our-new-future.aspx (2020).

Phillips, J. Travel trends in 2021: what to expect from the future of travel after Covid-19. https://blog.smartvel.com/blog/travel-trends-in-2021-what-to-expect-from-the-future-of-travel-after-covid-19 (2021).

Pineda, D. Amanda Gorman translation backlash sparks racial controversy. *Los Angeles Times*, 22 March 2021. www.latimes.com (2021).

Pulliam-Moore, C. https://splinternews.com/how-woke-went-from-black-activist-watchword-to-teen-int-1793853989 (2021).

Ranger, S. What is Hyperloop? Everything you need to know about the race for super-fast travel. www.zdnet.com/article/what-is-hyperloop-everything-you-need-to-know-about-the-future-of-transport/ (2021).

Rayan, A. www.edexlive.com/opinion/2018/sep/07/why-its-important-to-use-gender-neu tral-language-3877.html (2020).

Rayan, A. OED word of the year expanded for 'unprecedented' 2020. www.bbc.co.uk/news/entertainment-arts-55016543, 23. 11. 20 (2020).

Roberts, S. www.bbc.com/culture/article/20190314-how-brexit-changed-the-english-language (2020).

Schweiger, A. https://sprache-im-lockdown.uni-graz.at/de/ (2021).

Steffens, D. 20 Jahre Mauerfall – Zur Wortschatzentwicklung seit der Wendezeit. https://core.ac.uk/download/pdf/83653613.pdf (2020).

Websites

www.airfrance.fr (2021)

https://aircanada.com (2021)

www.annaheger.de/pronouns/ (2021)

www.atanet.org/ (2021)

www.bbc.co.uk/news/newsbeat-50052420 (2020)

www.bbc.co.uk/news/world-us-canada-50239261 (2021)

www.bbc.com/culture/article/20190314-how-brexit-changed-the-english-language (2020)

www.bbc.com/worklife/article/20170329-the-hidden-sexism-in-workplace-language (2020)

http://bei-uns-sind-hunde-freunde.de/erneuter-shutdown/ (2021)

www.bfmtv.com/economie/pourquoi-le-teletravail-ne-prend-plus-en-france_AN-2021020402 54.html (2021)

www.birminghammail.co.uk/news/local-news/jajo-the-rabbit-hired-as-translator-at-birm ingham-180747 (2020) www.bl.uk/russian-revolution/glossary (2020)

www.bmj.com/content/368/bmj.m447 (2020)

www.britannica.com/topic/social-change (2020)

www.britannica.com/science/binomial-nomenclature (2020)

www.btb.termiumplus.gc.ca (2020)

https://business.toutcomment.com/article/on-dit-madame-le-juge-ou-madame-la-juge-13369.html (2020)

www.chefdentreprise.com/Thematique/digital-innovation-1074/Breves/L-evolution-des-technologies-sans-contact-apres-le-confinement-352718.htm (2021)

www.ciol.org.uk/ (2021)

www.ciol.org.uk/cpd/other-workshops (2021)

www.cit-asl.org/new/wp-content/uploads/2018/12/f-Relay-interpreting-IJIE-10-2.pdf (2020)

www.collinsdictionary.com/dictionary/french-english/journalier (2021)

www.connexionfrance.com/Mag/Language/12-Arabic-words-used-in-French (2020)

https://core.ac.uk/download/pdf/83653613.pdf (2021)

https://csa-research.com/Insights/ArticleID/536/machine-based-interpreting (2020)

https://deepl.com/en/translator (2021)

https://devforum.zoom.us/t/multiple-incoming-and-outgoing-languages-for-interpreters/19178 (2020)

https://dictionary.cambridge.org/dictionary/english/pod (2021)

https://dictionary.cambridge.org/dictionary/english/permissive-society (2020)

www.dw.com/de/der-duden-modernisiert-sich-und-mistet-aus/a-54559347 (2020)

www.education.gouv.fr/bo/21/Hebdo18/MENB2114203C.htm (2021)

www.elmundo.es/cultura/literatura/2020/11/24/5fbcf1eefc6c83351e8b4577.html (2021)

http://emilyrussellhistoryinternal.weebly.com/the-rainbow-warrior.html (2020)

https://english.stackexchange.com/questions/305305/is-there-a-term-for-the-use-of-adjectives-as-nouns (2021)

https://en.wikipedia.org/wiki/List_of_German_expressions_in_English (2020)

https://en.wikipedia.org/wiki/Telenovela (2020)

www.europassitalian.com/learn/history/ (2021)

www.everything2.com/title/neo-patriotism (2021)

www.expansion.com/opinion/2020/11/26/5fbed8b9468aeb33738b4647.html (2021)

www.explainthatstuff.com/linearmotor.html (2020)

www.faz.net/aktuell/rhein-main/frankfurt/sperrstunde-in-frankfurt-ein-weiter-weg-zur-neuen-normalitaet-16989279.html (2020)

https://francais.rt.com/france/77206-rassemblement-manif-pour-tous-devant-assemblee-nationale-contre-projet-loi-bioethique (2020)

www.france24.com/en/france/20200605-french-connections-la-covid-19-how-coronavirus-has-affected-the-french-language (2020)

www.france24.com › 202103. Covid-19: la Chine lance « un passeport santé » numérique (france24.com) (2021)

www.france24.com/en/20121206-tintin-congo-not-racist-belgian-court-rules (2021)

www.francetvinfo.fr/sante/hopital/la-nous-sommes-vraiment-embolises-aux-urgences-usagers-et-professionnels-de-sante-tirent-la-sonnette-d-alarme_2664446.html (2021)

www.frenchbee.com (2021)

www.genderleicht.de/Textlabor/genderstern-nach-umlaut (2021)

www.geo.de/wissen/24003-rtkl-sprachpolitik-ein-mieter-ist-maennlich-der-duden-streicht-das-generische (2021)

www.ghd.com/en/about-us/ten-emerging-trends-shaping-our-new-future.aspx (2021) https://globalvoices.org/2020/09/11/are-romance-languages-becoming-more-gender-neutral (2021)

www.gov.uk/government/publications/guidance-for-interpreters/guidance-for-interpreters (2020)

www.governo.it/it/articolo/comunicato-stampa-del-consiglio-dei-ministri-n-90/16024 (2021)

https://hbr.org/2011/11/the-power-of-a-first-name (2020)

www1.ids-mannheim.de/ (2021)

https://ids-pub.bsz-bw.de/frontdoor/deliver/index/docId/6433/file/Steffens_Von_Pseudoa nglizismen_2017.pdf (2020)

https://ilbolive.unipd.it/it/news/ritiro-ghiacci-norvegia-rivela-unantica (2020)

https://interpretershelp.com/ (2020)

www.IRIS-Akademie.de (2021)

www.iti.org.uk/resource/spring-pulse-survey-shows-improved-market-conditions.html (2021)

www.jhsph.edu/covid-19/articles/achieving-herd-immunity-with-covid19.html (2020)

https://journals.sagepub.com/doi/abs/10.1177/0022009414538476 (2021)

www.juriterm.ca (2020)

https://languages.oup.com/google-dictionary-en (2020)

www.larousse.fr/dictionnaires/francais/pulv%C3%A9riser/65074 (2021)

www.larousse.fr/dictionnaires/francais/mill%C3%A9nial/188370 (2021)

www.lemonde.fr/international/article/2020/06/19/la-vie-des-noirs-compte-proclame-le-pa rlement-europeen-dans-une-resolution_6043520_3210.html (2020)

www.lemonde.fr/m-perso/article/2020/04/27/lundimanche-aperue-coronabdos-les-nouvea ux-mots-du-confinement_6037915_4497916.html (2020)

www.lexico.com/definition/nouning (2020)

www.libertarianism.org/columns/anarchism-libertarianism-two-sides-same-coin (2021)

www.linguee.com/english-french/search?source=auto&query=the+event+finale (2020)

www.linguism.co.uk/ (2021)

mailchi.mp/literarytranslators/alta-statement-on-racial-equality-in-translation (2021)

www.merriam-webster.com/dictionary/demographic (2020)

www.merriam-webster.com/words-at-play/prohibition-era-words/booze-cruise (2020)

www.merriam-webster.com/words-at-play/prohibition-era-words/speakeasy (2020)

www.mutualart.com/Article/A-New-Era-for-Auctions-/E7D86FE1C5916EC8 (2020)

https://mymemory.translated.net/en/Spanish/English/enfeudamiento (2021)

https://ngenespanol.com (2020)

www.omniamfg.com/mechanical/2020/10/20/how-things-work-the-hyperloop (2020)

https://onesmallwindow.wordpress.com/2019/07/18/where-is-the-privatisatio n-of-court-interpreting-heading/ (2020)

https://onzetaal.nl/taaladvies/engelse-werkwoorden-met-een-u-nederlandse-vervoeging/# close (2021)

https://otter.ai/ (2020)

www.owid.de Neuer Wortschatz rund um Corona (2021)

www.pastglobalchanges.org/people/people-database/index.php?option=com_comprofiler& task=userprofile&user=5355&lang=en (2020)

www.people.ku.edu/~a326m085/2019-ESA-Interstellar-BG.pdf (2020)

https://politico.eu/article/debate-over-gender-inclusive-neutral-language-divides-Germany (2021)

https://public.oed.com/updates (2021)

https://publications.parliament.uk/pa/cm201213/cmselect/cmjust/645/64508.htm (2020)

www.repubblica.it/economia/rapporti/osserva-italia/trend/2020/04/20/news/il_retail_dop o_il_covid_19_sei_tendenze_per_i_consumi_della_fase_2-254514182 (2021) https://resources.german.lsa.umich.edu/vokabeln/deutschhilftenglisch (2020)

www.royalairmaroc.com (2021)

https://secretsoftheice.com/climate/glaciers (2020)

www.servimedia.es/noticias/1335401 (2021)

https://slate.com/human-interest/2013/10/cool-the-etymology-and-history-of-the-concept-of-coolness.html (2020)

www.spanishdict.com/translate/articulo (2021)

www.spektrum.de/news/der-eisige-pass-der-wikinger/1723096 (2021)

https://sprache-im-lockdown.uni-graz.at (2021)

https://techforword.com (2020)

https://termcord.eu (2021)

www.theguardian.com/world/2020/may/13/le-la-covid-coronavirus-acronym-feminine-academie-francaise-france (2020)

www.theguardian.com/lifeandstyle/2019/dec/25/woke-to-gammon-buzzwords-by-people-coined-them (2020)

www.theguardian.com/travel/2009/jul/15/learn-italian-phrases-football (2021)

www.theguardian.com/media/2020/jun/20/associated-press-style-guide-capitalize-black (2020)

www.theguardian.com/society/2020/feb/03/being-woke-isnt-so-easy-even-if-you-know-what-it-means (2020)

www.theguardian.com/world/2021/feb/23/from-coronaangst-to-hamsteritis (2021)

www.theguardian.com/science/2020/nov/01/secrets-of-the-ice-unlocking-a-melting-time-capsule-archaeology-glaciers (2021)

www.topendsports.com/sport/extinct/harpastum.htm (2020)

www.translationdirectory.com/glossaries/glossary330.php (2021)

www.un.org/en/gender-inclusive-language (2021)

www.wipo.int/edocs/mdocs/aspac/en/wipo_ip_cmb_17/wipo_ip_cmb_17_3.pdf (2020)

www.wired.co.uk/article/what-is-the-gig-economy-meaning-definition-why-is-it-called-gig-economy (2021)

www.wur.nl/en/Research-Results/Research-Institutes.htm (2020)

www.youtube.com/c/techforword (2020)

www.youtube.com/hashtag/bbclearningenglish (2021)

www.yourarticlelibrary.com/philosophy/7-major-factors-that-influences-socio-cultural-changes/84824 (2020)

www.zdnet.com/article/what-is-hyperloop-everything-you-need-to-know-about-the-future-of-transport/ (2020)

Articles from the Institute of Translation and Interpreting Bulletin

"A world of change" by R. Schwartz et al., *ITI Bulletin* Jan–Feb 2015.

"The mysteries of transcreation" by Toby Bristow, *ITI Bulletin* May–Jun 2017.

"Terms of endearment" by S. Bassnett, *ITI Bulletin* Jul–Aug 2018.

"Beyond machine translation" by Jost Zetzsche, *ITI Bulletin* Mar–Apr 2019.

"CHDICT lessons" by Gábor Ugray, *ITI Bulletin* Sep–Oct 2019.

"Machine translation beyond post-editing" by Jost Zetzsche, *ITI Bulletin* May–June 2019.

"Time to get creative" by Jost Zetzsche, *ITI Bulletin* Jan–Feb 2020.

"Not in front of the children" by C. Storey, *ITI Bulletin* Jan–Feb 2020.

"Online assistance" by Akiko Sakamoto, *ITI Bulletin* Mar–Apr 2020.

"In at the deep end" by Rosie Dymond, *ITI Bulletin* May–Jun 2020.

"Transcreation demystification" by Toby Bristow, *ITI Bulletin* May–Jun 2020.

"As the crow flies" by Radhika Holmström and Radhika Menon, *ITI Bulletin* May–June 2020.

"Moving forward" by Kerry Gilchrist et al., *ITI Bulletin* Jul–Aug 2020.

"Distanced voices" *ITI Bulletin* Jul–Aug 2020.

"Weird and wonderful CPD" by Dean Evans, *ITI Bulletin* Sep–Oct 2020.

"The translator's kitchen diaries" by Hannah Lawrence, *ITI Bulletin* Nov–Dec 2020.

"Ethics and machines in an era of new technologies": ITI research e-book 2019.

"Negotiating a new path", ITI e-book published online on 1 February 2021 and edited by Catherine Park.

INDEX

Note: page numbers in **bold** indicate a glossary entry.

Milton Keynes UK
Ingram Content Group UK Ltd.
UKHW022011100124
435826UK00003B/8